PLOT *versus* CHARACTER*

A BALANCED APPROACH TO WRITING GREAT FICTION

JEFF GERKE

WRITER'S DIGEST
BOOKS
WritersDigest.com
Cincinnati, Ohio

For more resources for writers, visit www.writersdigest.com/books.

To receive a free weekly e-mail newsletter delivering tips and updates about writing and about Writer's Digest products, register directly at http://newsletters.fwpublications.com.

14 13 12 11 10   5 4 3 2 1

Distributed in Canada by Fraser Direct
100 Armstrong Avenue
Georgetown, Ontario, Canada L7G 5S4
Tel: (905) 877-4411

Distributed in the U.K. and Europe by F+W Media International
Brunel House, Newton Abbot, Devon, TQ12 4PU, England
Tel: (+44) 1626-323200, Fax: (+44) 1626-323319
E-mail: postmaster@davidandcharles.co.uk

Distributed in Australia by Capricorn Link
P.O. Box 704, Windsor, NSW 2756 Australia
Tel: (02) 4577-3555

Library of Congress Cataloging-in-Publication Data
Gerke, Jeff.
  Plot versus character : a balanced approach to writing great fiction / by Jeff Gerke.
    p. cm.
  Includes bibliographical references and index.
  ISBN 978-1-58297-992-2 (alk. paper)
  1. Fiction--Authorship. 2. Fiction--Technique. I. Title.
  PN3365.G47 2010
  808.3--dc22
                          2010021923

Edited by Scott Francis
Designed by Jessica Boonstra
Cover image by Rudi Tapper/istockphoto.com
Production coordinated by Debbie Thomas

DEDICATION

To my youngest daughter,
Sophia Song Taylor Gerke

© Mary DeMuth

ABOUT THE AUTHOR

Jeff Gerke is a novelist and professional book doctor. He is popular at writers' conferences across America as a fiction teacher. His style is informal and droll and tends toward the speculative. Jeff spent twelve years on staff at various publishing houses before launching his own small publishing company, Marcher Lord Press, in 2008. He writes under the pen name Jefferson Scott having authored such books as *Virtually Eliminated*, *Fatal Defect* and the Operation Firebrand series. His also the author of *The Art & Craft of Writing Christian Fiction*. Jeff and his wife of more than twenty years have three children.

TABLE OF CONTENTS

★ ★ ★

INTRODUCTION

***

Oh, ma hon-ey, oh, ma hon-ey, bet-ter hur-ry and let's me-an-der
Ain't you go-in'? Ain't you go-in'? To the lea-der-man, rag-ged
me-ter man?
Oh, ma hon-ey, oh, ma hon-ey, Let me take you to Al-ex-an-der's
Grand stand brass band, ain't you com-in' a-long?

They may not look like much, but these simple words sparked a revolution.

The year was 1910 and a young man named Israel Isidore Baline had written his first song, an instrumental march song called "Alexander's Ragtime Band." He was a Jewish immigrant from Russia now living in New York and trying to make it on the Broadway scene.

"Alexander's Ragtime Band" got picked up by a Broadway producer and played a few times in his "Folies" [sic] show. But the song failed to impress audiences. After a handful of performances, it was dropped from the show. Baline's first song was finished. In his own words, he considered it "a dead failure."

Six months later, perhaps out of boredom or desperation, he penned lyrics to the song. They were simple words. Lowbrow, in the estimation of some. About a mundane topic: Someone taking a date to hear a band play a new musical fad.

Come on and hear! Come on and hear! Al-ex-an-der's rag-time band!
Come on and hear! Come on and hear! It's the best band in the land!
They can play a bu-gle call like you nev-er heard be-fore
So nat-u-ral that you want to go to war

That's just the best-est band what am, ma hon-ey lamb
Come on a-long, come on a-long, let me take you by the hand
Up to the man, up to the man, who's the lead-er of the band
And if you care to hear the Swa-nee Riv-er played in rag-time
Come on and hear, come on and hear,
Al-ex-an-der's Rag-Time Band.

Despite the poor grammar and trendy topic, the words resonated with listeners. Suddenly the song was in demand throughout Broadway and beyond. In a day without Facebook or Twitter, "Alexander's Ragtime Band" sparked an almost overnight international dance craze—and sent its composer on a meteoric rise.

Soon everyone knew his name. Only he wasn't going by Israel Isidore Baline anymore. He had since changed it to the more American-sounding Irving Berlin.

Berlin now had the chance to show he was no one-hit wonder. In his sixty-year career he wrote an estimated 1,500 songs and the scores for nineteen Broadway shows and eighteen Hollywood films, including eight that received nominations for Academy Awards. Songs he wrote include "White Christmas," "Puttin' on the Ritz," "There's No Business Like Show Business," and "God Bless America."

And it all started because he added words to his little ragtime march.

"Irving Berlin has no *place* in American music," composer Jerome Kern later said, "he *is* American music." Composer George Gershwin called Berlin "the greatest songwriter that has ever lived."

Irving Berlin was astonished at his sudden rise to fame. As he reflected on why "Alexander's Ragtime Band" had failed at first and later succeeded, he came to a conclusion: "For music to live, it must be sung."

MUSIC AND LYRICS:
TWO TYPES OF NOVELISTS

Nothing changed about Irving Berlin's tune when he wrote the lyrics. But it wasn't until words were added that it became something magical.

Often a piece of writing can be brilliant in one area but lacking in another. Until that other area can be improved, the project will remain "a dead failure."

This is just as true in writing fiction as it is in writing music.

I believe there are two types of novelists, i.e., two archetypes into which all fiction writers may be grouped. On the one hand you have those for whom *plot* ideas come naturally. On the other, you have those for whom *characters* arise with ease.

Plot-first novelists think of story ideas all day long. Theirs are the fabulous books in which many exciting things happen. The focus tends to be on the events occurring in the story rather than on the characters, and usually, lots of things blow up. I know about this kind of novelist because I'm one of them.

Character-first novelists are those writers who are endlessly fascinated by what makes people tick. The fictional people they create are rich, engaging, believable, and compelling. You feel that those people truly exist.

The problem is that each kind of novelist is usually as awful at the one thing as she is terrific at the other thing. The plot-first novelist tends to create characters who are flat, unrealistic stereotypes: cardboard cutouts who, despite different moods, agendas, genders, and occupations, seem eerily similar to one another—and the author's personality. The character-first novelist produces wonderfully vibrant characters—but often has no idea what to make these interesting people do. Rarely do you see a novelist who is naturally good at both. I have never met one.

What's a writer to do?

In music, people solve this dilemma by finding a partner who is good at what the other is weak in. So you get Rogers & Hammerstein, Gilbert & Sullivan, Lerner & Loewe, Menken & Ashman, Berstein & Sondheim, and Webber & Rice. One brings the music and the other brings the lyrics. While it works great for music, it's a bit more cumbersome when writing fiction.

There have been examples of novelists cowriting success-ful books. Stephen King and Peter Straub, Larry Niven and Jerry Pournelle, and Margaret Weis and Tracy Hickman come to mind. The best-selling *Left Behind* series was written by coauthors Tim LaHaye and Jerry B. Jenkins. LaHaye supplied the theological leadership and left most of the actual writing to Jenkins.

By and large, though, writing a novel is a solitary thing. It is an effort most often engaged in by an individual author sitting alone at her laptop dreaming the most incredible dream.

IN A PERFECT WORLD

Ideally, you would have been born with twin gifts: The ability to create magnificent characters and the ability to originate thrill-ing, satisfying stories that act as stages upon which these char-acters can prance.

Chances are, you were not thus born.

As you've read the introduction so far, you've probably been able to figure out which category you belong to. You've been told, "You write like a guy," by which the person usually means you come up with great explosions but boring people, or "Well, you've got … good dialogue," by which the person means she was bored silly but liked your characters.

Maybe you think you're in a category not yet mentioned. I've had people tell me they are setting-first novelists. They mean they come up with ideas for the *place* before anything else. But I contend they are 1) really thinking of plot ideas triggered by a location or 2) really thinking of the setting as a character. Which means they're still in my two groups. I've had one author tell me she was a murder-first novelist. She meant she came up with the murder first and then the story spun out from that. Okay, but the murder is a plot idea, so she's still a plot firster.

Some novelists don't think it's important to improve the area they're weak in. I know from my own experience that most plot-first novelists don't think it's necessary to create realistic characters. I mean, so long as the chick is next to the truck when it blows up (in order to make the hero mad so he'll go off and do the next plot point) we're golden. Characters are like pieces of furniture to these writers. George Lucas talks about his characters in *Star Wars* as pieces on a chess set. He moved them around until the story was what he wanted. Is it any wonder characters by these writers sometimes seem as if they're cardboard or simple stereotypes?

Character-first novelists, on the other hand, can sometimes lift their noses at those crass brutes who want to write only about explosions and mayhem. They're more interested in the relationship dynamics between the mother and daughter. Now, on some level these authors may feel a quiet desperation and a certainty that their books aren't really going anywhere. But adding plot structure would not be their first choice for a solution.

For music to live, it must be sung. Without lyrics, many a tune will remain just a little ditty. Without music, lyrics are just a poem.

For fiction to be strong, it must include both engaging story and intriguing people. You must be utterly convinced of this or there's no point in you reading farther.

As a plot-first novelist, you have to believe that spending the hours and days it will take to create realistic characters is vital. It is every bit as essential to the success of your book as is the scene in which the spy infiltrates the villain's lair. You would take days or weeks to get that scene exactly right, wouldn't you? Assign that much importance to doing the hard work of character creation, and you'll be sitting pretty.

As a character-first novelist, you have to believe that you are not a sellout to pop culture if you create something interesting for your characters to do. It is not formulaic writing to craft a satisfying, page-turning structure for your book. If you don't do the unintuitive (for you) work of constructing this framework, no one will have the joy of meeting your characters. And you can have the confidence that your book will move briskly and tie everything off.

I know you're good at one and not so good at the other. You recognize that, or you wouldn't have picked up this book. I applaud you for being willing to step up to the plate and say, "Okay, this is a weak area for me, but I'm going to listen to what you have to teach. I'm here to learn."

The beauty of *Plot Versus Character: A Balanced Approach to Writing Great Fiction* is that it gives both writer groups what they love—and gives it back and then some.

The character-first novelist will discover that a solid plot structure for her story will result in a resounding amplification of what she wants to do with her fictional friends. Her characters will never be so perfectly displayed as when given the backdrop of a strong plot. And the plot-first novelist will discover the personal delight in having realistic characters peopling her bang-up story. Her plot will resonate to the deepest parts of the reader's psyche when acted out by unforgettable characters.

Ah, bliss.

It may not spark an international dance revolution, but it will make your fiction imminently readable, enjoyable … and publishable.

A BIT ABOUT ME

I don't know if you're like this, but when I read a nonfiction book I want to know who this person is who thinks he has the authority to stand up and try to teach me something. If it's a subject I care deeply about, I really want to know the credentials of the author. So, here goes.

I entered the publishing industry in 1994 when I got my first three-book deal to write a trilogy of techno-thrillers. When that contract was completed, I took a job as an editor at the publisher that had produced my novels. I worked there until going freelance in 2002, at which point I got my second three-book deal, this time for a trilogy of military thrillers.

I then took a position at another publisher, where I was able to spearhead the launch of a fiction line—specifically for a niche of science fiction and fantasy. During this time I was also writing and cowriting nonfiction books. In 2005, I moved to a third publishing company to manage their fiction line.

At every point in my career I was acquiring fiction of all genres—historical novels, chick-lit, southern gothic, police thrillers, and more—but I've always had a special place in my heart for weird fiction. So I acquired science fiction and fantasy and other off-the-map genres whenever I could, and launched the careers of some best-selling speculative novelists along the way. (So if my examples in this book tend more toward *Star Wars* than *Wuthering Heights*, I hope you'll forgive me!)

I've loved teaching fiction since the first writers' conference I ever attended, way back in 1999. I had never been to one, and there I was teaching the continuing track for fiction. It was incredible, and I've been exhorting novelists like you ever since.

I continue to teach at several writers' conferences every year. My online Fiction Writing Tip of the Week column formed the basis of my first craft book, *The Art & Craft of Writing Christian Fiction*. I have developed a number of writer's helps products, including interactive systems called *How To Find Your Story* and *Character Creation for the Plot-First Novelist*.

In the book you hold in your hands, I draw from all of that content and add more, to construct the complete model for how to achieve the perfect balance between fully realized characters and fully actualized plots.

A PLAY IN THREE ACTS

Plot Versus Character is laid out in three sections. Part 1: Building Your Characters takes you through my detailed system for creating realistic story people. Part 2: Building Your Plot shows you how to construct brilliant plots for your characters to cavort within. And Part 3: Bringing It All Together covers how to integrate it all into your novel.

Since you probably already know which type of writer you are, you may be tempted to jump to the section covering your area of weakness. You can certainly do so, of course, but I urge you to read the book from cover to cover. This is an interrelated system and each principle builds upon the previous one. To actually use this material, you need to have read it all. And you never know, you may find something in the section covering your area of strength that will help you do it even better.

THE CURTAIN RISES

Here's what Irving Berlin wrote about the song that catapulted him to stardom: "The melody started the heels and shoulders of all America and a good section of Europe to rocking. The lyric, silly though it was, was fundamentally right."

Whether you're strongest as a plot writer or a character writer, that part of it is your melody. It might start some heels and shoulders to rocking. But if you stop there, if you remain satisfied with that, your story will never sing. You're reading this book because you are courageous. You are willing to do the work to add the other part, the part that doesn't come easily to you, to make your story fundamentally right.

Let's start making music.

I

DOES IT REALLY MATTER?

— ★ ★ ★ —

ASK A PROFESSIONAL TENNIS PLAYER IF SHE NEEDS a good backhand or if a strong forehand will suffice. Ask a professional musician if it would be better to sing or play an instrument only or if being able to do both well will help his career. Ask a doctor—or, better yet, ask patients—if it's enough for a surgeon to have a great bedside manner or if it would also be good if she's skilled with a scalpel.

Consider the legendary actor James Earl Jones, the voice behind Darth Vader and Mufasa the lion. He was blessed with this rich, booming voice, and yet he had a serious speech impediment that manifested at age five. His stutter was so severe he refused to speak aloud, and he remained functionally mute until he reached high school. In college, he focused on acting because he'd found he loved it. He could've been content to just stutter his whole life, but the success he dreamed of in the field he had chosen would've remained forever out of his reach.

So it is with you.

I have no doubt that you are naturally gifted with either a strong sense of story or an endlessly bubbling brook of character ideas. Every novelist I've met has come equipped with one or the other, standard. The corollary is that you're probably pretty weak at the thing on the other side of the coin.

Yet you sense that it isn't enough to go with your strengths and just overlook your weaknesses as a novelist, or you wouldn't have picked up this book. I applaud you for your courage. Most people don't want to take the time to buttress their sagging foundations. They're intimidated by what appears to be an unreachable goal—or they simply haven't figured out yet that they have a problem. Not so with you.

FICTION LITE

But is it really that big a deal? I mean, a golfer with a great long game but horrible putting still has a great long game, right? He won't win any tournaments but he'll probably draw the cameras for his tee shots. That should be enough.

I suspect you sense something wrong with that approach. You don't want to do well in only half the skill set. You want to take home the trophy.

Let's look at the two kinds of novelists.

CHARACTER-FIRST WRITERS

A novelist with a talent for creating marvelous *characters* will populate her book with fascinating people and sparkling dialogue, and that should satisfy any reader. Right? Don't we come to fiction to meet interesting characters we'd like to get to know in detail?

Following that theory, we get long, tedious passages like this:

"So ye think it's all destined, do ye? A man has no free choice at all?" He rubbed at his mouth with the back of his hand. "And when ye chose to come, for Brianna, and then again, for her and the wean—it wasna your choice at all, aye? Ye were meant to do it?"

"I—" Roger stopped, hands clenched on his thighs. The smell of the *Gloriana's* bilges seemed suddenly to rise above the scent of burning wood. Then he relaxed, and gave a short laugh. "Hell of a time to get philosophical, isn't it?"

"Aye, well," Fraser spoke quite mildly. "It's only that I may not have another time." Before Roger could expostulate, he went on. "If there is nay free choice … then there is neither sin nor redemption, aye? … We chose—Claire and I. We wouldna do murder. We wouldna shed the blood of one man; but does the blood of Culloden then rest on us? We wouldna commit the sin—but does the sin find us, still?"

"Of course not." Roger rose to his feet, restless, and stood poking the fire. "What happened at Culloden—it wasn't your fault, how could it be? All the men who took part in that—Murry, Cumberland, all the chiefs … it was not any one man's doing!"

"So ye think it is all meant? We're doomed or saved from the moment of birth, and not a thing can change it? And you a minister's son!" Fraser gave a dry sort of chuckle.

"Yes," Roger said, feeling at once awkward and unaccountably angry. "I mean no, I don't think that. It's only … well, if something's already happened one way, how can it happen another way?"

"It's only you that thinks it's happened," Fraser pointed out.

"I don't think it, I know!"

"Mmphm. Aye, because ye've come from the other side of it; it's behind you. So perhaps *you* couldna change something—but I could, because it's still ahead of me?"

—Diana Gabaldon, *The Fiery Cross*

On the one hand, it seems okay. It's a good exchange. There's a strong feeling for distinctiveness between the two characters. Some snappy banter. But ... nothing happens. Yakety-yak-yak.

It might seem unfair for me to lift a random page of dialogue and expect it to have pyrotechnics or at least a good bar fight. But this goes on through the entire book. Read this from an Amazon reader's review of the book quoted above:

> As I was reading this book, I was trying to figure out why it was so tedious and hard to get through. I am an avid reader. I read every night. I feel that if I can get through a James Michener novel I can get through anything. ... One problem apparent to me was that there were no feelings of "I can't put it down, what happens next? I can't turn the page fast enough" in this book. ... So what was it then? ... the plot? Maybe that was the whole problem. The plot was poor and boring, almost nonexistent.

Ouch. Space does not permit me to include long passages from this novel in which the characters are dealing with the minutia of everyday life, including potty training a child, brewing coffee, and noticing the many kinds of weeds found in a forest. According to another reviewer, "The remainder of the book is filled with excruciating and repetitive (albeit generally well-written) detail about mundane aspects of the main characters' lives over a very short and largely uneventful span of time."

In other words, good characters—good writing, even—but nothing happens. It's a snoozer. That's what you get when you score A+ for your characters but get an F for plot.

Have you felt that way about your own writing? You know you've got great characters and some terrific scenes, but you have this lingering foreboding that nothing is happening. Worse, you don't know what to do about it. You think maybe a subplot or a kidnapping or … I know: a new character! Even as you think it, you realize you're grasping at straws. So your book gets longer and longer but never seems to find its way home.

PLOT-FIRST WRITERS

On the other hand, maybe you're a plot-first writer. You never have a problem driving your plot home. In fact, you probably drive *over* any actual character who dares try to arise from the bubbling asphalt of your story. Plot firsters steamroll their way from plot point to plot point, cloning characters on the copy machine in the sky and cracking the whip to make them do whatever it is the plot needs them to do next.

What do we get when we score an A+ for plot and an F for characters? We get *Cliffhanger* and *Mission to Mars* and *The Transporter 2*. And we get the character named Levine in Michael Crichton's *Jurassic Park* sequel, *The Lost World*.

For pages, this character goes on and on about the sanctity of maintaining a pristine environment in the lost world. And he is a meticulous scientist. For instance, we get this commentary from the narrator:

> The truth was that Levine—brilliant and fastidious—was drawn to the past, to the world that no longer existed. And he studied this world with obsessive intensity. He was famous for his photographic memory, his arrogance, his sharp tongue, and the unconcealed pleasure he took in pointing out the errors of colleagues. As a colleague once said, "Levine never forgets a bone—and he never lets you forget it, either."
>
> Field researchers disliked Levine, and he returned the sentiment. He was at heart a man of detail, a cataloguer of animal life, and he was happiest poring over museum collections.
>
> —**Michael Crichton**, *The Lost World*

Fastidious. Critical of others for their sloppiness. Okay, that works as a partial character sketch. But ask yourself, would that person do the following:

> Thorne shrugged. He still saw nothing. Standing behind him, Levine began to eat a power bar. Preoccupied with holding the binoculars, he dropped the wrapper on the floor of the hide. Bits of paper fluttered to the ground below.
> "How are those things?" Arby said.
> "Okay. A little sugary."
> "Got any more?" he said.
> Levine rummaged in his pockets and gave him one. Arby broke it in half, and gave half to Kelly. He began to unwrap his half, carefully folding the paper, putting it neatly in his pocket."
>
> —**Michael Crichton,** *The Lost World*

Levine did what? This wild-eyed scientist/activist, whose only semblance of an actual personality was that he was obsessed with keeping man's impact on nature to nil, drops a candy wrapper to the ground? It's incredible. It's unconscionable. It's completely wrong for that character.

But, you know, the author needed a reason for the dinos to eat him.

That's why this is called *character-serving plot*. It's such an egregious example of character-serving plot that I use it as my prime example whenever I teach at conferences. Who cares that this character would never do such a thing? The plot must be serviced!

Do all your characters feel pretty much like you? Oh, I know that every character we write is, in a sense, a manifestation of ourselves, but that's not what I'm talking about. It's not enough that your characters differ from you in terms of gender or motive or background or race or externals like that. Do you have this sense that your characters are either just like you—in how they talk, think, etc.—or are mere stereotypes?

Here's a test: If you refer to your characters as "the girl," "the boss," "the fat guy," and "the villain," you might be a plot firster. If you accidentally switched the names of two of your characters and no one could tell the difference, you might be a plot-first novelist. If you find yourself able to, with little effort, make it Fred who defuses the bomb instead of Mike, you might be a plot firster.

But who cares, right? It's a great story. People will be entertained. They'll never guess what's going to happen, but when they find out they'll feel like it was the right call. What more can anyone ask? Certainly there are plenty of successful novelists and filmmakers who create stories that are all about plot. *First Blood,* anyone?

You hear a higher music, though. You're not content to write cardboard characters or you wouldn't be reading this book. Though you sense it will be difficult to create characters as wonderful as your plots, you realize your fiction could achieve another level entirely if you did, so you're willing to give it a try.

DISCIPLINED AND READY TO WORK

And it will be hard. Whether you're a plot firster learning to create differentiated characters or a character firster learning to write solid plots, it's going to be work. After all, doing something you're not naturally good at is hard.

In school, I was an A student in every subject—until I hit foreign language classes. I took French in high school and found it baffling. Suddenly I understood what it was to be at the rear of the class. Then in college, I was forced to take a foreign language again. Thinking that maybe I was just no good at Latin-based languages, I signed on for two years of Russian and worked my tail off to scrape by with a B-. I had to work a lot harder for that B- than most of the other students had to work to get an A. It simply did not come easily to me.

So it is with you and the part of writing you're not naturally good at. It's so hard to create good characters if you're a plot-first novelist, and vice versa. In the past, if you've tried to get better at that thing, you may have felt like you were banging your head against a wall. The effort may have actually hurt your brain, almost as if you had a physical brain block that you wouldn't dare approach, much less try to scramble over.

Happily, you've now found *Plot Versus Character,* and I will show you how to achieve balanced fiction without needing a frontal lobotomy. It will still be hard work and not entirely within your comfort zone, but it will be possible. And much more pleasant than two years of Russian, I assure you. Da, ochen.

OH, THE RANCHER AND THE COWMAN CAN BE FRIENDS

Literary critics would like us to believe that character-driven fiction is superior to plot-driven fiction, that it is the only sort worth taking up shelf space. They revere Jane Austen and Anne Tyler and J.D. Salinger and tilt their virtual noses above Dan Brown and Harry Turtledove and countless other (usually better-selling) plot-first novelists.

So which is better: character-first fiction or plot-first fiction? I have come to believe that the answer is *yes.* Both.

The Holy Grail of fiction is to write the novel with the perfect balance of character and plot, of memorable people and a stirring story. The reader cares for these people and is desperately engaged in what they've been caught up in.

I recently introduced my teenage daughter to the movie *Casablanca*. Now there is a story that struck the balance. Is it character driven or plot driven? If anything, it tips a tad toward being character driven, but what would it be without the tightening noose of the Nazis? If Victor Lazlo weren't running from Hitler's hounds, what would drive the story forward? What would give it its suspense? What would be the stakes? Without the fascists, they could sit around drinking Señor Ferrari's excellent coffee and just be interesting characters together.

Or take Bernard Cornwell's *The Winter King*. It's a brilliant retelling of the Arthurian legend set in historical England after the withdrawal of the Romans. His Arthur, Merlin, Guinevere, and Derfel (his narrator) are wonderfully drawn characters. But if there had been no Saxons to unite or battles to be fought, the book would've failed. It is the conflict and epic action that define and propel these characters. Without it, they wouldn't have been heroic at all.

My own *Operation: Firebrand* series follows a group of friends in their various arcs and relationships—all while performing high-tech covert ops in the world's hot spots. I was going for that perfect blend of character and plot.

I set myself a challenge when I sat down to write the first *Firebrand* novel. Could I, a card-carrying plot-first novelist who had already written a trilogy of plot-driven novels, write a character-driven (or at least character-*influenced*) series of novels? Could I even create realistic, layered, memorable, believable characters? Could I pull off a whole story that allowed those characters to be true to their personalities, or would I sacrifice who they were to serve my plot?

What I learned in the process became the basis for this book. I learned that a plot-first novelist could, if sufficiently motivated, learn to write strong characters whose selves were not violated by the needs of the plot. A little later I realized that character-first novelists could learn to write breathtaking, satisfying, page-turning plots, as well.

The trick is to teach each kind of novelist how to gain strength in the area they are weak in by using techniques they are already naturally good at.

So the character-driven novelist learns how to create plot by *finding the story from within the main character.* And the plot-first novelist learns how to make realistic characters by *finding the plot of the main character's change.*

That's what we'll be doing in this book. I hope you'll read it from start to finish and not just jump to the part you feel you need the most help with. This is a system with two major components, but they can't be taken in isolation. They build upon one another.

The character-first novelist will find herself in familiar territory as we start, because I base everything on the main character's inner journey. That magnificent—or tragic, or both—transformation that makes the heart of the character-first novelist sing. The plot-first novelist will find himself on solid ground too because I approach this inner journey in plot terms, with clearly defined waypoints that will make sense to the plot writer.

Then, when we move to creating the plot, once more you'll feel at home no matter which kind of novelist you are. The character-first novelist will feel less threatened because the plot is nothing more than an amplification of the main character's inner journey. The story is the stage upon which the character shows her true self. The plot firster will feel comfortable here too, not only because it's his native land, but also because he suddenly realizes that this "character thing" is actually helping him accomplish his plot and story goals.

The plot firster uses plot-first tools to create amazing characters and the character firster uses character-first tools to fashion incredible plots. Everybody wins, everybody delights his or her audience, and nobody has to venture far out of his or her comfort zone.

A WORD ABOUT MALE AND FEMALE NOVELISTS

You may have detected a trend in my examples above. Most of the plot-first novelists I've referred to have been men and most of the character-first novelists I've referred to have been women.

As stereotypes go, this one has at least one use. Limited, perhaps, but use nonetheless. Generally speaking, women are often more interested in people and relationships and men are typically more interested in things happening. Women tend to prefer getting together to chat, while men would rather go off and do something together.

There are many exceptions to this, of course, which is why the stereotype has only limited merit. My wife and I are opposites, in terms of the typical male-female roles. I'm the talker and she's the doer. It's a struggle to get her to share her feelings, whereas I'm likely to express my feelings to anyone passing by.

The stereotype doesn't hold true for novelists across the board, either. When I teach in writers' conferences I describe plot-first novelists and character-first novelists and then have the attendees raise their hands to classify themselves into one group or the other. For character-first novelists, I'll usually get 75 percent of the women and 25 percent of the men. The same is true but opposite for the plot firsters: 75 percent of the men and 25 percent of the women.

We have more Tom Clancys than John Irvings, after all, and more Nora Roberts than Doris Lessings.

Don't worry if you're a woman who comes up with story ideas before character ideas, or if you're a man who cares more deeply about the people you create for your book than what the book itself is about. Male or female, you're either a plot-first novelist or a character-first novelist, and this book will help you with the part that you're not naturally good at.

TIME TO VENTURE FORTH

There's no shame in admitting you need help. The shame would be from not getting it.

No matter how strong your free throws, if you can't dribble and pass you'll never make it in the National Basketball Association. No matter how well your fingerwork is on the French horn, you'll never make the philharmonic if you can't stay on pitch or tempo.

We're going to start by building terrific characters. If you're a character firster, I urge you to read this section and not skip over it. My system for building characters is a bit different from every other book or system you've encountered, and you might just like my way.

If you're a plot firster, put on your thinkin' cap and roll up your sleeves, put your nose to the grindstone and break out the elbow grease, because you're about to get suddenly good at the thing you've been weak at your whole writing career.

Every novelist can become a better novelist by seeking that elusive harmony between brilliant characters and breathless plot. And when you achieve it, your fiction will really sing.

Part 1

MEMORABLE CHARACTERS

P*lot Versus Character* is more about building usable characters and stories than it is about theory. When you get to the end of *Plot Versus Character,* if you've done the steps suggested along the way, you will have a living, breathing main character *and* a terrific story framework built around her. You will have, in short, everything you need to begin writing your book—including the part you may have never had before.

In this system, everything rests on your main character. The plot arises out of the main character. The genre and background and era might even be chosen to better enhance what you're wanting to do with your main character. Consequently, we're going to start by building your protagonist. (You will want to go through part 1 for the top three to six main characters in your book, but all of them take a backseat to your hero or heroine.)

"Part 1: Memorable Characters" builds character on the *Shrek* model: Ogres are like onions. Or in our case, wonderful characters for fiction are like onions. They're layered. Here are the layers we'll build your hero from:

CHARACTER LAYERS

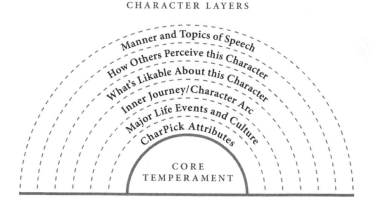

A glance at the on the previous page diagram reveals that the nucleus of any fully realized character is her core personality. That's the topic of chapter 2.

But to differentiate your characters realistically, you don't stop there. We add layers. These layers are what distinguish two characters who might have very similar core personalities. They might both have the same basic temperament but they will not be identical in the other layers. They'll be so different, if you work this system as outlined, that an observer wouldn't be able to see that they shared the same core personality until he got to know them much better.

The heart of your character *as it pertains to this story* is his inner journey. We'll find his personality core first, then we'll add some decoration or costuming, and then we'll trace out the steps of his character arc. At the end of the section, you're going to be itching to get this character on stage.

As you move through part 1, keep a pencil and paper (or laptop) at the ready. You're going to be building your protagonist as you go, one layer at a time.

2

CORE PERSONALITY

★ ★ ★

ARE YOU JUST LIKE ANYONE ELSE? I MEAN JUST LIKE, as in no one including your mother could tell you apart from the other person?

I'm guessing not. Even identical twins are different from one another—though on the genetic level they are technically clones. The closer you look the more differences emerge. No two people are identical.

So why do we see novels peopled with identical characters? Why is there so little variation or even creativity between characters in so many novels?

Oh, sure, the characters in these novels might be different on the surface. One is male and the other is female. One is old and the other is young. One is Asian and the other is Caucasian. One has long hair, tats, and sundry piercings while the other is a choir boy with a crew cut. But these are just costuming issues. They hardly distinguish personality.

Ideally, they are an *expression* of personality, but that's not the same.

Then you get differences in attitude. One is mean and the other is nice. One is anxious and the other is relaxed. One is bitter and the other is forgiving.

Or differences in agenda. One is after someone's job and the other is content where he is. One wants to have a baby and the other wishes she could get rid of her nine kids.

Sometimes you see differences in speech that the author hopes will constitute the person's entire character: the surfer dude and the low rider and the butch and the New Ager and the hillbilly.

Blech. Even taken together, these things do not add up to a *personality*—neither in fiction nor in life.

Worse, we often see outright stereotypes in fiction. The kindly old man, the rebellious teenager, the floozy, the greasy politician, the authoritarian military man.

But even if you had an angry floozy with red hair, an Australian accent, and the goal to sleep her way up the corporate ladder, you still don't necessarily have a real character.

Without selecting a core personality for your characters, most likely all the people in your book *will feel the same.* The peaceful ex-Marine with a lisp and the desire to just get by on the minimum may, to the author, seem different from the floozy, but at his core, at the spot where his actual personality should shine through, he will feel just like the floozy to the reader. As will the crook, the pedophile, the mailman, and the FedEx clerk.

Because without an authentic character personality, no amount of external decoration can conceal the fact that the mannequin under it all is the same mannequin under all the others.

The difference these characters is lacking, the difference your characters must have from one another, is core personality.

GETTING TO THE HEART OF
THE MATTER

When I had set myself the challenge to create an ensemble cast of characters for my *Operation: Firebrand* novels—and succeeded in landing a three-book publishing contract to bring these people to life—I pretty much panicked.

What have I gotten myself into? I don't know how to make differentiated characters! Think, Jeff, think. How do you make characters seem different? Well, who studies differences in character? Psychologists. Yeah, yeah! I'll run to the bookstore and look up personality types in the psychology section. Psychologists are supposed to know what makes people tick—and what makes them different. And wait, I've done those personality self-tests before. I'll look into those too.

I walked out of the store with a book worth its weight in gold, if you'll excuse the cliché. I found it in the psychology section. It's a temperament studies book called *Please Understand Me II* by David Keirsey. Though it is not a book designed for novelists, novelists can gain a great deal from it. In it, Keirsey works with the Myers-Briggs temperament classifications.

The thing that separates *Please Understand Me II* from other books based on the Myers-Briggs model is that Keirsey describes how these temperaments will behave in so many arenas: career, marriage, hobbies, parenting, conversation, and more. Keirsey describes in marvelous detail what each type aspires to, what kind of language each type uses, what type of work each type gravitates toward, and which type-to-type pairings work best (and worst) in relationships. Lots of grist for the novelist's mill.

The Myers-Briggs model divides all personalities into four broad categories, and further divides each category into four subcategories, resulting in sixteen possible character types. These types are the inspiration for the way we'll develop characters in *Plot Versus Character.*

You don't need to use *Please Understand Me II*—or even the Myers-Briggs temperaments. But you need to find some model to serve as the basis for your characters' core personalities. The entire system depends upon it.

A couple of other great resources that cover personality types—and are more geared to novelists—are *45 Master Characters* by Victoria Schmidt and *The Writer's Guide to Character Traits* by Linda Edelstein, Ph.D.

Now, using a personality type for the basis of your character may not sound very impressive to you. You may find yourself saying, if we're using stock characters, how can we create original characters for our fiction?

Well, there's a bit more to it than that. Recall the Character Layers graphic on page 23. A character type represents a core temperament, but then you add layer upon layer to round out your character and bring your fictional person to life. As we'll see, beginning in the following chapter, no two characters built in the way you're going to build them will ever be the same, even if they're based on the same temperament type.

SOME TEMPERAMENTS

Let's begin, shall we? Your first step in creating a character is to choose a core personality temperament. I'm going to assume here that you're building your protagonist, but the principles apply to all your major characters. You don't have to go through the entire process for every character in your novel, by the way, just the top three to six.

You can use any examination of personality types to help you do this. As I've stated, my preference is for the Myers-Briggs model and I highly recommend adding a copy of *Please Understand Me II* to your personal fiction craft library.

Let's look at a brief explanation of the Myers-Briggs model to get an idea of how to begin forming a core personality type for your character. As you read through these descriptions, keep in mind the character you're creating. Which of these types seems closest to what you want to do with this character? Remember, you're not trying to find yourself in these descriptions (although it might be good for you to do that once, just to get it out of your system), but to find your character in these descriptions.

The Myers-Briggs Type Indicator (MBTI) categorizes all personality types in terms of four dichotomies, or either-or choices. Everyone, for example, is either an extrovert or an introvert. That's one of the four dichotomies. The other three either-or dichotomies are sensing vs. intuition, thinking vs. feeling, and judgment vs. perception.

From these, the Myers-Briggs system assigns letters:

- Extrovert (E) or Introvert (I)
- Sensing (S) or Intuition (N)
- Thinking (T) or Feeling (F)
- Judgment (J) or Perception (P)

According to the system, everyone is on one side or the other of each of these little seesaws. Someone might be an extroverted, sensing, thinking, judger (ESTJ) or an introverted, intuiting, feeling, perceiver (INFP) and so forth. There are sixteen possible combinations of the letters and traits.

That means there are sixteen core personality types. As we've seen already, that doesn't mean there are only sixteen possible characters for use in fiction. Though, speaking of my own particular weaknesses, having sixteen differentiated characters in my beginning fiction would've been a sixteen-fold improvement!

THE SIXTEEN TYPES

Here are brief summaries of the sixteen Myers-Briggs personality types. These only scratch the surface. You will get a much fuller description of personality than space allows me to provide here. I recommend you use one of the books mentioned in this chapter or find another source to help you select your main characters' core personality types.

- INFP—Sees the world as full of wonder, as through rose-colored glasses; must have work that has a meaningful purpose; idealistic.

- ENFJ—Organized and decisive; works to build harmony in personal relationships; empathetic; sees potential in everyone.

- ISFJ—A serious observer of other people; overwhelming desire to serve others; often taken advantage of; responsible.

- ESTP—Tolerant and flexible; actions, not words; the doer, not the thinker; spontaneous; impulsive; competitive.

- INFJ—True activist for a worthy cause; good insights into other people; remembers specifics about people who are important to him.

- ESTJ—The person self-appointed to keep everyone in line; prefers facts to opinions; stays with the tried and true; practical.

- ENFP—Idea person; warm and enthusiastic; enjoys work that involves variety and experimentation.

- ISTJ—Quietly thorough and dependable; always seeking to clearly understand things; punctual to a fault; can seem cold.

- ESFJ—Generous entertainer; lover of holidays and special occasions; natural leader; good delegator; encourager; cooperative.

- ENTP—Ingenious; outspoken; easily bored by routine; challenges status quo; institutes change; clever; incisive.

- INTP—Obsessed with achieving logical consistency of thought; natural and creative scientist; looks for the logical explanation.

- ENTJ—Organizes groups to meet task-oriented goals; vision caster; always seems to find himself leading; spots inefficiencies and fixes them.

- INTJ—System builder; both imaginative and reliable; natural strategist; long-range planner; independent and original.

- ISTP—Doesn't do something unless it's a big project into which he can throw himself utterly; great "big problem" solver.

- ESFP—Exuberant; outgoing; a lover of life; hedonistic; partier; scattered; into things that are "new"; Johnny on the spot; chatty.

- ISFP—Sensitive; caring; all about feelings: his and other people's; moody; quiet; kind; doesn't like conflict; needs his own space.

HOW TO PICK YOUR
CHARACTER'S TEMPERAMENT

As you've read through those descriptions, I hope you were able
to see one or two that might work for the character you have
in mind. Follow up by reading the fuller descriptions in *Please
Understand Me II* or another resource.

When I'm creating a new character, I turn to *Please Understand Me II*. The author has grouped the sixteen types into four
main temperament groups. I read those general group descriptions first. Usually doing that will get me into the neighborhood
of what I'm sensing this character should be.

Then I'll dig deeper by reading the four types within the
main category I've selected. Again, I'll keep reading until I get
an internal check that says, "Nah, that's not her." If I get all the
way through the description without finding anything that triggers that internal check, I know I'm on to something. Indeed,
most times I'll encounter one or more items that ring true about
this character. I'll go, "Yes! That's totally her!"

Whether you use the Myers-Briggs model or some other
study of character type, reading the general descriptions will
help narrow your search. You can then dig deeper to find more
traits that fit your character until you have a match.

Once I have a match, I begin writing notes. You might not
do it this way, but I like to write down or type up what parts of
that personality description really resonate with me about this
character. I may not know how I'll use the idea in the story—I
might not even know what my story is yet!—but I know I'll
want to work it in somehow because I've found something that
is intrinsically, almost poetically *right* about her.

If you're a plot-first novelist and you experience one of these
Zen-like moments of rightness, you will find yourself oddly

geeked over something you'd never given a great deal of thought to: characters. And then you're hooked.

I said before that if you follow this system thoroughly you won't end up with characters who are the same, even if they're based on the same temperament. That's because you'll be reading through the type descriptions with a different person in mind each time. For instance, as you're trying to find the core personality of your mother character, different parts will jump out at you than the parts that will jump at you as you read through thinking about, say, your second lieutenant character in Vietnam. It will never be like the same description twice.

USING YOUR OWN TEMPERAMENT

If you're like most novelists, you'll automatically base your protagonist on *yourself*. It's certainly an understandable temptation.

But I would advise you to not choose your own temperament for your main character—at least for the first few times through this system.

The problem with basing your protagonist on your own personality type is that you can't really see yourself. You are the least objective person on the planet when it comes to the subject of you. You may perceive yourself as outgoing and fun, while the whole rest of the world sees you as the antisocial toadstool you really are. (I'm joking, here, but you get the point.)

And if you don't have a clear sense of who you are—and, let's face it, most people do not—how can you write a consistent fictional character if that character is based on yourself? When it comes to writing characters for your novel, one of your largest blind spots is most likely your own personality.

If you simply must use yourself as the main character, then study the description of that type carefully. Be sure you're adhering to how your personality type normally behaves, even if *you* wouldn't do it that way. Once you step off that path, internal consistency of character will forever elude you in your novel and you won't even know where you lost it, much less how to get it back.

Also, if you decide to use your own temperament for the hero, don't let any other character in the book have the same temperament. You'll need to raise a barrier around your protagonist, metaphorically speaking, to make sure you don't ooze out into the personalities of one or more (or all) of the other characters in your book. We plot firsters already know how to make every one of our characters seem the same. What we need is to learn how to make them distinct from one another.

COMMENCE LAYERING

If you haven't already chosen a base personality type for the character you're building, do so now. Everything that follows in this book builds on this.

If you're having trouble choosing between two or three, just pick one of the candidates and run with it. If you find yourself scrunching your face and thinking, *That really doesn't seem like her,* then go back and try one of the other candidates.

In a pinch, you can always take a bit of one of the types to add to another type that the character seems most like, because real people sometimes score highly on two or more types. But it will make it harder to keep track of who this person would really be and how she would really behave. Since that's the thing plot-first novelists most need, I don't recommend you combine types. At least not with your first set of characters built using this book.

When you settle on your type for your character, take a good long time to go back through the description, writing down ideas that occur to you based on those details. Note how this person behaves in public, what she aspires to, what she'd like to be seen as, what she values, what types she best gets along with, what types rub her the wrong way, what careers she would gravitate to, what kind of spouse and parent she will be. The works.

Make notes like crazy for how these things could come into play in your story. You may not use them all in the book, but they'll get you in the right frame of mind for who this person is.

Then, equipped with this ocean of thought about this character, you can come back and soak in it as you're writing. Losing touch with who this person is? Come back to these notes and bask awhile. Wade around in the ideas you first had that gave you those a-ha! moments as you dreamed her up.

All of the character work we'll do from here on finds its origin in the core personality. Don't move ahead until you feel you know this person in her essence. You should be able to reach the point where you can spot her personality type at a party or in conversation. When you know her that well, you're ready to add the next layer.

Through the rest of part 1, we'll be not just layering elements on top of this core, we'll be tracking how this core temperament *expresses itself* through the ensuing layers. Everything else is seasoning applied to the meat (or soy product) of your choice: fish, chicken, pork, beef, lamb, or octopus. The central ingredient remains the same no matter what you add to it, but how that flavor is skewed or tweaked depends on what comes next. Always begin with the core and look for how it would work itself out through the layers applied on top of it.

3

PHYSICAL AND NATURAL ATTRIBUTES

* * *

IN REAL LIFE, THE FIRST THING WE NOTICE ABOUT people is their physical appearance. Gender, ethnicity, age, height, build, hairstyle, clothing style, attractiveness, etc.

In fiction too these things are important. Indeed, they are among the factors that differentiate characters who have the same core temperament. Let's say you meet two people with the same personality type, but one is an old man from Taiwan and another is a teenage girl from the Bronx. If you were to hang around them both for a good long time, you might begin to sense the similarities in their personalities, but you would certainly not notice those things right away.

Plot-first novelists tend to begin their character work with physical attributes and leave it at that. Yeah, he's the tall guy with the Amish beard and she's the beautiful blond with the legs. That doesn't work so well—not if you want to create realistic characters. But neither can you neglect appearance.

Physical attributes are kind of an outside-in approach to characters. The previous chapter is an inside-out approach. Both are important. And even this chapter doesn't end with appearance. We'll also be talking about natural attributes—as in *aptitudes*—and "accidents" of birth, such as family of origin, birth order, gifts and talents, and more.

What we're talking about here is what this character was given at birth and in the intervening years that put a spin on the core temperament and make this person unique.

As you go through this chapter, keep an eye out for physical attributes that might better express who this person is at her core. Here are a couple of examples using the Myers-Briggs model:

- A character of the ENFJ temperament (who would have a tendency to be highly organized) has a tattoo diagram on her wrist that explains something important to her so she'll always have it "on hand."

- An ESTP (a temperament that lends itself to spontaneity and competitiveness) character wears the most fashionable clothes and is constantly getting compliments for his taste and style.

Further, look for ways that this character's core temperament would adapt to the physical "costume" and background God gave her. For example, an ENTP character (who based on their temperament would be naturally inventive and clever) from a very poor family might've learned six ways from Sunday to get old cars to work, to get free cable, and to generate electricity from a *Gilligan's Island*-style bicycle generator.

Do you see how everything grows out of the core tempera-ment? We don't pick one and then forget about it as we move on. We find the ways that this core temperament is adjusted and finds expression in everything else.

This chapter consists of a large number of categories for you to consider as you design this character: eye color, health, edu-cation level, etc. As you go through picking out what you want for this character, keep her temperament in mind.

Don't think anything you choose here is set in stone. If you give him a massive scar across his forehead but then later real-ize that someone of his temperament type would've had that removed long ago, go back and change it. This process is to get your creative juices flowing about this person, not to hinder your creativity. Let it enable, not disable, you.

First, the physical attributes. Then we'll talk about talents and upbringing.

PHYSICAL ATTRIBUTES

What does your character look like—and why?

GENDER

You might think this a no-brainer, but at least let your mind consider what this character would be like if the gender were opposite to your first inclination. Playing against type—a female bouncer at a club or a male nanny—might be fun.

RACE AND ETHNICITY

Think beyond the obvious here. If you've got an ENTJ character (a personality type known to take charge of situations), what if you made her of a minority ethnicity or an enslaved people group? How would her natural leadership express itself within such confines?

Think also about the cultural distinctives inherent in the race you choose for this character. Is he a Hispanic low rider, an African-American rapper, an Asian scientist? Now, of course we're flirting with stereotypes, so be careful to avoid that. But if a character is of a certain temperament and has certain aspirations, he might choose or identify with one of these types to achieve some goal. You'll have to work hard to express his personality in spite of the type, but it should still be an option for you.

If your character is in high school, you almost have to choose a type! Jock, druggie, geek, skater, Goth, goody two-shoes, whatever. As any member of those subgroups can tell you, there's a wide variety of personalities possible within any of them, but to an external observer they may all look exactly the same.

Think also about the impact this character's culture would have on her. Does she come from a loud and voracious Italian family? Is she a repressed Jew? Is she driven to work extra hours from her Puritanical work ethic? Does she think she's nothing but white trash because that's what she grew up in? What are the cultural values and tendencies that might impact how her core temperament expresses itself? Again, seek to avoid stereotypes but be aware of the influence these cultures may have on your character.

What pressures are on this character because of her ethnicity? Is there a pressure to excel—or to underachieve? Is there pressure to go into a certain line of work or to pursue, or avoid, an education of a certain type? Are there restrictions on her activities or friends or choices of mate, due to her ethnic background?

How does this character fit within her race or ethnicity? Does she prefer interracial mingling or does she like to flock with birds of her feather? Is race even an issue for her?

AGE

How old is your character?

Answer both in terms of his objective age and his subjective age. In other words, he can be forty-two objectively and subjectively he can be "too old" for whatever he's doing, say, working in an ice cream shop.

As you think about *this* core temperament arising from *this* cultural background, how old should he be for the context you're placing him in?

It's a great thought experiment to at least consider that this character might be the "wrong" age for whatever he's doing—a Doogie Howser child prodigy or an octogenarian going back to college. Most of your characters will be pretty much the age they should be for what they do, but sometimes it's fruitful to investigate alternatives.

Here, as with all of your choices, keep this main question in mind: Can I better do what it is I'm wanting to do with this character if I make a different choice here?

PHYSICAL ATTRACTIVENESS

Despite our many protestations that we shouldn't judge a book by its cover, we all do. Certainly that is true of how we evaluate people. Beautiful women find doors opening for them that are not open to their less objectively attractive sisters. Characters with deformities, especially of the face, may make others feel uneasy and may therefore not achieve as they otherwise might.

How attractive is this character? I'm talking about objective physical attractiveness, not the winsome worth of her soul. When seen by people in the culture she finds herself, how do they respond? Do they find her attractive or not? And if yes or no, to what degree?

This necessarily includes things like the character's weight, height, measurements, and body mass index. In the eyes of this character's culture and era, is he considered attractive? Most people are not, by the way. Most people are plain, overweight, and out of style. So how does this character measure up?

Further, how does this attractiveness—or lack thereof—affect your character? If she is painfully aware of her homeliness, what does that do to someone of her temperament? Is she motivated to do anything and everything within her power to enhance her attractiveness, even to the point of paying for plastic surgery, or does she just not care? If he is attractive and he knows it, how does he take advantage of that to get what he wants? Or does he seek to even the playing field, perhaps by trying to look unattractive?

How athletic or fit is this character? Is he underweight? Overfed? Malnourished? Does he move with grace or all the elegance of a dinosaur with a destructo-tail?

What about posture? Does she slump? Has her neck become permanently bent forward over her protruding belly?

How does he walk? How does he stand and carry himself?

The physical attributes of a person have an impact on his personality—and even his prospects in life. The actress Kathy Bates will never play an ingénue. Brad Garrett will never play a jockey. We all find our place in the world based somewhat on how we look.

Similarly, sometimes a person changes his physical appearance to better match who he wants to be as a person. He might work out like crazy to have a sculpted body. She may undergo plastic surgery to better accomplish her goals (or avoid her fears). Perhaps your character is a woman who had felt powerless in her developmental years, and so as an adult she is well over three hundred pounds. She is no longer a pushover, literally or figuratively—and that could match the stubbornness in her personality. (But avoid making that the sum total of her character.)

FACE, HAIR, EYES, AND COMPLEXION

Take a minute to think about how this person's face should look. What color are his eyes and hair? Depending on ethnicity, you may not have a lot of variety here, but it's still worth considering.

Where you will have more wiggle room is in hair*style*. How does she wear her hair—and why? Is it long or short, curly or straight, up or down? Is it trendy or counter cultural? Buzz, punk, eighties, or old-fashioned? Bald by choice or comb-over nightmare? Natural color or from a bottle?

As always, keep this character's temperament in mind. How would an ESTJ (a temperament that tends to be very practical) wear her hair? Probably something no-nonsense. But an ESFP (someone who is very outgoing) might wear it as crazy as possible, something that says party animal.

Factor in the character's culture too and whether or not he wants to fit in to that culture.

Consider facial hair (speaking primarily about men, but you never know…). Artistic? Goatee? Lamb chop sideburns? Soul patch? Hitler moustache? Hillbilly beard—neck and all? Clean shaven? Three-day growth? What about the texture and color of it? Salt-and-pepper? A shock of bleach blond? What is he trying to say with this facial hair choice?

What about complexion? Does he have Edward James Olmos's craggy face or Orlando Bloom's glossy skin? Speaking again of ethnicity, is she darker or lighter than most of her sisters? Are there freckles or zits? Scars? Wrinkles? These things will affect a character's personality. A teenage boy with more zits than face probably will be beaten into such shame in the house of pain that is high school that it will permanently change who he is.

What shape is her face? One of those exotic elongated faces or a wide moonpie face? High cheekbones? Jutting chin? Dimples? Cleft chin? Prominent eyebrow ridge? Go to the mall and marvel at the many face shapes passing by you. Pick one for your character.

CLOTHING AND STYLE

What look is your character going for? Even in a fantasy, science fiction, or historical novel, there is room for statement in a person's attire, and this is certainly so in a contemporary story.

Is he trying to look like a cowboy? Does she dress to kill or dress for success? Does he just throw on whatever doesn't stink? Does she shop at The Gap or Neiman Marcus, or Walmart? Is there an elegance to her outfits? Is he always trying to get away with wearing jeans and tennis shoes, even at formal events? Is he going for the Hells Angel look?

In addition to clothing preference and goals, consider how *successful* the character is at achieving the targeted look. He may think he's the trendiest thing next to Johnny Depp, but in reality it's all schlock. She may be going for Halle Berry but ending up with Franken Berry. Or he may just be throwing on anything but ending up with an accidental dashing look that goes right along with the rest of his personality. Stripes and plaids mixed? An apparent color blindness? An affection for polyester?

Think about jewelry, hats, scarves, shoes, iPods, and other accessories. If it's not a contemporary story, think about weapons and armor and gadgets she might be wearing, and why.

What is your character trying to say or achieve or make others believe by how he or she dresses, why is he or she trying to do this, and how successful is the effort?

OTHER PHYSICAL CONSIDERATIONS

Here's your chance to describe anything else about this character's physical appearance that a bystander would notice. Does he walk with a limp? Is she missing a fingertip? Does he have a birthmark? Is one side of her slightly larger and longer than the other? Does he have an especially large or small head? Many people are taller than you when standing but shorter than you when sitting at the table. They're long in the legs but short in torso. Others are the other way around.

Don't leave this section until you could give a police artist such an excellent description of this character that it would lead to an arrest.

NATURAL ATTRIBUTES

Now it's time to look at this character's inherent gifts and background. These things are typically less visible but equally or more powerful to how the character behaves. Keep his temperament in mind as you consider these options: How would someone with that personality core react and adapt, given these accidents of birth?

FAMILY OF ORIGIN

Into what kind of family was this character born? Was it a large family with seventeen children and four generations living in the same house? Was it a one-child, single-parent dad living in a mansion in Beverly Hills?

Were the character's parents married when she was born? Did they stay married throughout her development? Was it a second marriage and a blended family? Was it a marriage in name only? Was it a happy, stable home?

What was the level of wealth of the family he grew up in? Was he accustomed to privilege or poverty? Does she know her way around a yacht club or a nightclub? Were they on food stamps or welfare? Did they help out the "underprivileged"? Did he grow up on the wrong side of the tracks or did he go to all the right schools?

Whether she was, as a child, more accustomed to advantage or squalor will have a large impact on her attitudes, expectations, and knowledge set. Choose these things consciously, in ways that will amplify or play against her temperament.

Think about birth order. I'm not a devotee to the idea that firstborns are always smarter and middle children are always peacekeepers and so forth, but I do believe it has some impact. It does something to you when you're suddenly in a position to care for someone smaller than you in your family—and when you're no longer the sole object of your parents' affection. It does something to you to be the only girl in a family of six males.

So for your character, consider birth order and number, gender, and relative ages of siblings. Where did he fit in? How would someone with this temperament be if she were the baby in a family of seventeen?

Did your character have a parent or family member with an especially strong (or weak) personality that greatly affected this character? Who was it and what was the effect?

Where did your character grow up? Was her dad in the military and so they lived all around the world but never more than two years in any one place? Did he grow up in the hills of Kentucky or the streets of the Lower East Side? Is she a Valley girl or country girl? We'll talk about manner of speech in a later chapter, but certainly your character's speaking, accent, and colloquialisms would be affected by the region from which she hails. So, where does your character hail from?

What else about this character's family of origin has impacted the man he's become? We'll talk in the next chapter about major life events, so for now I want you to think just about the effect your character's family history has had on him.

Think about people you know. Remember the Nordic guy from Minnesota? He was a product of his upbringing. Or what about the Chinese girl who had been adopted by Caucasian parents—how would her life have been different if she'd grown up in Henan Province instead of Colorado? These nature vs. nurture issues are what we're looking at here. How has this character's family of origin impacted her personality?

EDUCATION AND INTELLIGENCE

How well-educated is this character? Grammar school or graduate school? Even if you're writing a fantasy or historical novel, you can give a relative education level for your character.

The question isn't just the level of the person's education but the quality of it. Someone with a doctorate in thirteenth-century England might not know as much as someone with a sixth-grade education in our society today. A character with a diploma from the University of Phoenix might not be as valued in the marketplace as someone with a diploma from MIT or Harvard Business School.

So what is the education level—and quality—of this character? Given what you know about her upbringing, family wealth, culture, and temperament, how high would she have gone in education? How high would she have *wanted* to go? Did she study what she wanted to study or what she was expected to study?

Of course it's not the same as education, but how *intelligent* is your character? A highly intelligent character has a nobility of bearing that is born out in her actions and choices. And even someone with a Ph.D. can still be pretty dumb. When it comes to both mental acuity and common sense, how smart is this person? How will this level of intelligence bear out in her life? Given this intellect and this temperament, what can we expect to see?

GIFTS AND TALENTS

What is this character good at? By trial and error and through the feedback of others, we all gravitate toward the things we're naturally gifted in. In the best case, we can join the things we're good at with the things we enjoy doing and turn them into something we can make a living at.

What are your character's gifts and talents? Does he have a knack for fixing things? Does she have an ear for foreign languages? Can he sing to melt the hearts of any fair maid? Can she dance with the grace of flowing water? Does he have the uncanny—and sometimes unfortunate—ability to express his thoughts verbally? Can she read people almost like she's psychic? Does he have a gift for teaching or a way with animals? Does she cast visions that people will lay down their lives to achieve?

What is your character naturally good at? It doesn't have to be a superpower; in most cases, it should be something more subtle.

Also, what does this character enjoy doing? Does she love entertaining? Does he love working out the math and then handing the answer to the leader? Does she enjoy making things with her hands? Does he groove on influencing people to his point of view? And how good is this character at what he or she enjoys?

Usually what she enjoys and what she's good at are one in the same, but sometimes they aren't. She may love singing but be tone deaf. He may love children but end up scaring them off. Sometimes a character feels she could've been very good at something if given encouragement and half a chance. "Why didn't you make me stay with piano lessons, Mom?"

How is it with your character? What does he enjoy doing and how good is he at it?

Has she been able to turn these things into gainful employment, or is she still dreaming to go out on her own as a dance instructor or politician or missionary to Kenya?

LOVE LANGUAGE

A man named Gary Chapman has developed a theory of communication that I have found very useful for characters (and life in general). He calls it the five love languages.

The theory is that, like gifts and talents, each of us is born with a tendency to express and receive love in a certain way—in a love language—but that not all of us speak the same language.

Some of us understand love in terms of what we do for someone else. I'm saying I love you if I clean up your room or have your car fixed for you or make your dinner. I *receive* love—that is, I understand that you are saying you love me—when you do something similar for me.

But what if you don't speak my love language? What if you understand love in terms of gift giving? You say I love you when you bring me a rock you found that made you think of me or when you pick up a can of my favorite soft drink on the drive over, and you expect to receive love in like manner. So now I'm fixing your bathroom but you're giving me a rock. Both of us are saying I love you but neither of us is "hearing" the other correctly.

Enter Dr. Chapman with his *The Five Love Languages* books. If I can realize that you're not ignoring my expressions of love and are, indeed, expressing love back in your own way, many happy endings can be found.

Chapman says the five love languages are:

- words of affirmation—these folks say I love you by saying, well, "I love you," and "I appreciate you" and "thank you"; for them, it's all about the words expressing that they notice you and you are valuable to them;

- quality time—these people say I love you by giving you their undivided attention, by sitting beside you and being there for you, by putting everything else off to be sure you're okay;

- receiving gifts—these people say I love you by giving you thoughtful items; they effortlessly present gestures of affection and consideration to the people they love;

- acts of service—these folks say I love you by washing your clothes and fixing your computer and mowing your lawn; their love is active and shown in the many, sometimes overlooked, things they do for you; and

- physical touch—these are the huggers, the touchy-feely types who can't cross a room without having physical contact with others in some way; they express love by giving physical contact in caring ways.

It stands to reason that a person who gives love in these ways is predisposed to receive love in the same ways. A gift giver isn't naturally going to understand your undivided attention as love. Without Dr. Chapman's understanding, she won't "hear" your love until you give her some token of your affection.

Whether your character understands the five love languages or not, she will *have* a love language. Often an investigation of love languages will provide insight into how your character might behave in any given situation, how she will click with (or instantly dislike) someone else, or how there can be miscommunications.

Love languages aren't just for wooing and creating harmony. When a character (real or imagined) gets upset, *that's* expressed in terms of love language too. You know the hugger who won't touch you when she gets mad or the quality time person who won't look you in the eye or even stay in the same room with you to let you know something's amiss. You can see how the garbage or laundry would pile up if an acts-of-service person is upset. And that's just speaking domestically. Extrapolate out to villainous proportions and you have some cues for how your character will act if pushed too far.

Sometimes a character's love language is in perfect harmony with her temperament—like the outgoing ESFP who is a hugger, but sometimes it will not be a natural fit—like the introspective

INTJ who is also a hugger. These agreements or disparities can give you great ideas for complex characters.

I recommend that you identify your own love language. Understanding love languages can enhance or even save your dearest relationships. Plus, it's good for your fiction because if you're not being conscious about the love languages you select for your characters, you'll give them all the same one—yours— just by default.

SELF-ESTEEM

What does your character think about himself? Does he think he's God's gift to women or would he rather crawl into a hole and hide? Does she believe she has something to offer or does she sabotage all her relationships to verify her belief that she deserves nothing good?

It's time to play junior psychologist.

It may feel strange to think about a character's self-image. You might be saying to yourself, "This is a made-up character— how can she feel anything?" But you can't think that. You have to move from thinking of characters as props or furniture to thinking of them as real people.

Think about yourself. There may have been a time when you weren't the master and commander you are now. If you're like most people, you probably endured a time when you thought you were pretty worthless. (For most people it coincides with high school.) Then, through maturity and a growing sense of achievement, maybe you pulled yourself out of that feeling and now you believe you have something to contribute and you really are worth the oxygen you consume.

That elusive feeling of being normal, of being worthwhile and on an equal footing with everyone else—or that all too common feeling that is its opposite—is part of the experience of humanity. So this character under your microscope now will have dealt with it too. Will probably still be dealing with it.

So go Jungian or Freudian a moment and delve into the deepest psyche of your character (your *fictional* character). How does she feel about herself? Where does she think she ranks among her peers? Does she feel like she has the right to take up space? Has she always felt this way? Is she trending in a more or less healthy direction on this issue?

What were the milestones in his journey toward self-acceptance? What have been the blows that have kept him down? What lies does he believe about himself that keep him thus handicapped?

How is her achievement or lack of self-acceptance affecting her life? How does it affect the chances she takes or the things she says?

What would need to happen for him to reach a healthy self-image—or has he already attained it? Has he gone too far? Or is that apparent arrogance itself a compensation for feeling insignificant?

If you and I are at times tossed about by the powers of self-acceptance, surely a realistic character would be affected by them as well.

How is it with your character?

ZEAL

The last internal characteristic I want to talk about in this chapter is religious or other kinds of zeal.

Every person is passionate about something. Perhaps it's religion, perhaps it's politics, perhaps it's social activism, perhaps it's something else. Your character is passionate about something. Maybe she's consumed with protecting children from sexual abuse. Maybe he's fervent about organ donation. Maybe she marches for freedom of speech. Maybe he chains himself in front of bulldozers to protect the spotted tortoise. Maybe she writes letters to her Congressman about gun rights. Whatever it is, and to whatever extent it is, it colors your character's thinking and behavior.

Maybe the thing she crusades for isn't entirely clear to her. For instance, she doesn't know what apartheid is but she feels the need to protest it, and next week she'll protest something else. Because what she's really expressing is her dislike of conservative authority, and that actually stems from a rebellion against an autocratic father.

What is your character zealous about? Indeed, what is his religious orientation? Does he ascribe to any religion? Why? To what degree? How "religious" is he about his religion? If left to himself, would he still ascribe to this religion or is it something he's doing because of family or other pressures? What does he believe when he's alone?

Humans are religious. Even nonreligious people express the faith that there is no god or afterlife to concern themselves with. And those characters who aren't religious about religion are religious about something else. We all have zeal, and we all zealously express it at some time and in some way.

How is it with your character? If she had to fill in the blank in this sentence, how would she do so: "I love _____ enough to die for it"?

How will that zeal express itself in your character? Given his temperament and this particular zeal, how will it manifest?

CURRENT STATUS

Up to now we've looked at things that have gone into producing the character we want. We know where he was born, what his family life was like, what he's naturally good at, and how he expresses and receives love. Now it's time to look at how he is when the story begins.

How does the story find this character? Is he married? Divorced? Does he have kids? What's his level of wealth right now? Has he exceeded the expectations of his parents or has he pretty much done what they expected? Has he underachieved? What is his life situation right now?

How is she as a wife and mother? How is she doing in keeping herself in shape? How active is she in the community? What kind of employee is she?

Second, is your character happy with the current state of affairs? Given her temperament and upbringing and zealousness, is this pretty much where she thought she'd be at this point in her life? If not, what is still lacking or how has she surpassed her expectations? Is she content in her marriage or lack thereof? What are her current goals? What are her relationships with the family and culture of her origin? How has she used her gifts and passions? Is she still yearning to go to art school or seminary or to work with the Dalai Lama?

And here's something we haven't talked about before: morality. How moral is he? Is he meeting or failing to meet his own standards of right and wrong? Would his mother be proud of how he's living? What is his criminal record? How acquainted is he with the local jail or courthouse? Does he want his children to behave in ways other than how he behaves? Is there emotional and relational wreckage in his past? In his present?

Survey your character's life at the eve of the tale's beginning and write down how she is doing—and how she thinks she's doing.

COSTUMES

I love the fact that physical appearance impacts temperament. An ISFJ (a natural people pleaser) garbed in highly attractive physical features will be very different from another ISFJ who is garbed in low attractiveness. But under it all, the same diligent selflessness will remain.

Your task here is to take the core personality—the essence of this character—and "clothe" that person with a logical costume based on your choices as to her background and inherent talents and predispositions.

I hope you can see that you will never end up with two identical characters, even if they have the same temperament, and even if you stopped right here and didn't add the other onion layers.

This is hard work, I know. The plot-first novelist, especially, may find this grueling and may struggle to see the value of it. Just keep Irving Berlin's admonition in mind that for music to live, it must be sung. For your fiction to live, to "sing," you must populate your great stories with equally great characters. And that takes work.

4

MAJOR EVENTS, LIKABILITY, PERCEPTIONS, AND SPEECH

* * *

I TOOK A DEEP BREATH AND WENT TO FACE the mirror.

This is always the toughest part. Nearly two decades I've been doing this, and it still jars me to look into the glass and see a total stranger staring back. It's like pulling an image out of the depths of an autosterogram. For the first couple of moments all you can see is someone else looking at you through a window frame. Then, like a shift in focus, you feel yourself float rapidly up behind the mask and adhere to its inside with a shock that's almost tactile. It's as if someone's cut an umbilical cord, only instead of separating the two of you, it's the otherness that has been severed and now you're just looking at your reflection in a mirror.

I stood there and toweled myself dry, getting used to the face. It was basically Caucasian, which was strange for me, and the overwhelming impression I got was that if there was a line of least resistance in life, this face had

> never been along it. Even with the characteristic pallor
> of a long stay in the tank, the features in the mirror man-
> aged to look weather-beaten. There were lines everywhere.
> The thick, cropped hair was black shot through with gray.
> The eyes were a speculative shade of blue, and there was a
> faint, jagged scar under the left one.
>
> —**Richard K. Morgan,** *Altered Carbon*

Beginning to feel a bit like this guy? He lives in a future in which a person's consciousness can be transferred to new (or, as in the this case, *used)* bodies. As you start putting skin on this character you're creating, you're going to feel a little strange. Plot-first novelists, especially, aren't used to walking around in someone else's shoes. But as odd as it is, it's also invigorating.

At this point in the process you've gotten a fix on who this character is at her core, what she looks like, and quite a bit about what makes her tick: her family of origin, her passions, birth order, love language, talents, and more. We're headed to this character's inner journey, when all of these things will come into play. But first we need to add the final layers of the onion.

In this chapter we're talking about the major events in the character's life before the beginning of the story, how this character is likable (or at least understandable), how this character is perceived by others, and, lastly, how this character speaks.

THE IMPACT OF MAJOR LIFE EVENTS

Let's say you discovered the impossible: two exactly identical twins, duplicates in every respect all the way down to talents, predilections, and follicle count. I personally believe such a pair doesn't exist, but for the sake of argument, let's say you found the only extant instance.

Now separate them. One gets abducted and is raised by actors on the Lower East Side; the other is raised by his parents in their posh apartment. Think they'll still be identical?

Oh, they'll still look the same. They'll still be uncannily similar on many topics and areas of endeavor. Since they have the same core temperament (also not likely, but we're just playing here), they may be drawn to similar careers and hobbies.

But they will no longer be identical. The abducted one may feel that, at its base, the universe is unstable and unreliable—the entire framework of existence is liable to change without warning. What would that do to him? Would he be slow to commit to long-term relationships? Would he sabotage good jobs, feeling that it's better to strike than to be struck? Whereas his twin is happy to enter into a marriage with the best woman he can find, the wounded brother can't seem to find the right girl. Rather, he drives all the right girls away.

Even if you've managed to get this far in the process with two characters who are indistinguishable from one another, start adding the impact of major life events, and you'll begin to find your distinctions. Your twin characters may respond similarly to the events thrust upon them, but the events themselves will change the characters in fundamental ways.

PICK YOUR DISASTER

It's time to send your character through the wringer.

But picking major life events for your character doesn't mean you have to include earthquakes, wars, tornadoes, plagues, or sundry acts of God. What you're looking for here are major influences on this person's life—and then play them through the character's development right up to the moment the novel begins.

We've already touched a bit on the character's family of origin, especially the marital status of the parents. Think about that again here. A broken home is a big deal for a child. "Wait, I thought certain things were kind of set in stone. You're telling me they could change? They could end? Now I'm supposed to pick sides and love one of my parents over the other? Why does my world feel unsure? Why do I find myself getting in trouble at school all the time and being sad when it's Mom, not Dad, who comes to the principal's office?"

Walk this through in your character's life. Extrapolate from the event on through the character's childhood and all the way to the brink of the story. How would a character with this temperament and love language and the rest react to a broken home? What would it do to him? How would it impact his self-image and career choices?

What if the divorce happened later in life, when this character and all her siblings had left home? Would it undercut her assumptions about herself or would it not really faze her? What if there was a "new dad" and a blended family and suddenly she's not the eldest anymore?

The point is to drop a stone in the still pool of your character's life and watch the ripples.

Maybe the major event in your character's life was the loss of a sibling when they were both young. What if it was that he was born in a military family and every two years was torn away from whatever friendships he'd begun to develop? What if it really was a war or tornado or plague that traumatized the family? What if it was Mom slowly going insane? What if her parents abandoned her and she was left to take care of her siblings? What if Dad was never pleased with anything she did and she's been forever trying to make him proud of her?

What if, as in *My Sister's Keeper* by Jodi Picoult, your character discovers that the only reason she was born was to be a source of organs to be harvested and donated to a sibling? What would that do to a person?

You won't always find a major event of interest in your character's life. There may not need to be one. But it's a great avenue for your thoughts to travel down. As you play with possible major life events (and they can be good things too, like winning the lottery or becoming a movie star) and kind of toss them up against your character and his temperament and what you're wanting to do with him in this story, you may find something that sticks.

In my *Operation: Firebrand* novels I invented a major life event for my former Mossad agent, Rachel. As a little girl with her father, a hotelier in Tel Aviv, a Palestinian homicide bomber detonated his explosives in the lobby of her father's hotel. Her father and many others were killed in the blast. Little Rachel stayed by his body for hours before anyone found her.

As you can imagine, such an event forever altered the trajectory of her life. Gone was her childhood innocence. Gone was her conviction that all people were inherently good. Gone too was her father and the feeling of protection he had provided.

Now an adult, Rachel is not wholly defined by this experience. Her core temperament works its way out in everything she does. But she *did* become a Mossad agent working counterintelligence and she *has* constructed much of her look and manner so as to attract protector-type males. And she sometimes flies off the handle when children are orphaned or when she sees someone planning to harm civilians.

You see how one major life event can change a character's life and personality?

Consider yourself or people you know. Did you choose your line of work because of something that happened in your past? My wife and I adopted a little girl from China. She had cleft lip and palate, which has now been fixed but has contributed to a number of developmental delays in our daughter. Our older daughter was thirteen when we came home from China with her sister. She has been deeply involved in her little sister's therapies. Perhaps not surprisingly, she now wants to go to college to become an early interventionist specializing in toddlers with special needs.

A major event in her developing years has caused an important shift in her life's direction. Now, this isn't something out of the blue. It fits with our daughter's compassionate heart, love languages, and core temperament, so we think it may stick.

How many people went into medicine because they had a relative who died and they felt powerless to help? How many people go into a safety or law enforcement profession because someone they cared about was hurt and no one could do anything about it?

John Walsh, host of the long-running TV show *America's Most Wanted,* which has brought national exposure to missing and exploited children, was himself a victim—his six-year-old son was abducted and murdered and for years the perpetrator was not found. (Happily, the person behind this crime has now been identified and the case is considered closed.)

Major things that happen to us cause us to veer into directions we might not have otherwise gone.

Now it's time to think about this in relation to your character. Do you want him to behave in certain ways for the purposes of your story? Consider what major life event could've impacted him in such a way that he would naturally tend to do those things. Or maybe you want your character to be largely untouched by tragedies in the world, to be spoiled and even a little soft, so that when something major happens to her in the course of the story, she has no resources. She reels back for much of the story and has to eventually find a source of strength.

Take fifteen minutes to jot down a couple of dozen things that might've happened to your character at various junctures of his life. Follow each one through a couple of logical conclusions about how it would affect his character now that he's older. See if one (or more than one) of these might give you a wonderful surprise for this person.

When you find it, it'll make you eager to get to writing the book, I promise. But don't be hasty. Commit to work this system through to the end at least once before taking shortcuts.

LIKABILITY

If your book doesn't have a likable hero, your book is dead. End of discussion.

As an editor and book doctor I've seen countless (unpublished) manuscripts that begin with the protagonist in such a despicable state that the reader can't bear to stay in the story. These writers all had a good idea: to show a character who is very low so her rise to great heights is dramatic. But they started off with a character so low, so unlikable, that no one stuck around to see the transformation.

If the character you're crafting right now is your protagonist, you must make her likable in some way. You must achieve reader engagement with this character or the reader will leave. No one wants to commit to hanging around a distasteful person for three hundred pages. An endearing main character is one of the few must-haves for any novel to work.

But even if the character you're working on isn't the hero, he must still be likable—or at least comprehensible. Even the villain. Grendel's mother from *Beowulf* was a murderous monster who slaughtered an entire village—but she was also a female grieving the loss of her child. Don Corleone was a gangster and a killer, but oh how he doted on his grandchildren!

So for the character you're working on now, how is she likable or at least relatable? Because as soon as you start saying a character is purely this or utterly that, you've strayed into the land of stereotype. That's the death knell for this character's realism. Real people are complex. They have lots to like and lots to dislike. Characters with no gray areas, who are completely one thing, are boring and unrealistic. In other words, they're like the characters a plot-first novelist comes up with naturally. You've got to go beyond that.

Find something to like in your character. If it's your hero, find a *lot* to like about her. Begin thinking of ways to show this likability to the reader. But even if it's a minor character or a "bad" character, find the thing his mother could love about him, the thing a lover could hang all her hopes on that one day he will come back to the right path.

RULES OF ENGAGEMENT

To cause your reader to begin cheering for your hero, make her care about him. Make her engage.

Whom do we pull for? We tend to like the underdog, the guy who has the odds stacked against him but keeps bravely fighting. Is there a sense in which your character is an underdog? Could you portray that in an early scene? Maybe he's the only one who showed up to protest the opening of the new nuclear plant, but he's still valiantly handing out fliers. Maybe the girls in her class silently stand by while the mean girl knocks her books to the floor.

We feel for the downtrodden. We want to help. We want to see that person succeed. If you show your main character in a situation like that, you have instant reader buy-in.

We also like to pull for the person who is chasing a dream. The boy who finally gets his courage up to ask out the girl—and she laughs in his face and runs away. Ouch. The girl who has her debut ice skating competition and falls to her rump on the first required jump. Show your character trying to do or achieve something, especially if she fails at first, and your reader will be onboard.

We like people who are admirable, thoughtful, sacrificial, loyal, heroic, and moral. Show someone tripping an old man and we're not going to like her. But show the person coming to an old man's aid and you'll have us. Show a man buying flowers for his sweetheart. Show the woman with the chance to be on television who ends the interview early because her child needs attention. Show the man eyeing the sports car but driving away in the minivan. Show the woman who runs into the street to save a child from being hit. Show the little rich girl who goes to hold hands with the little poor orphan in the park.

We want to admire the person we're going to be spending all this time reading about. Compassion and friendliness and a lack of judgmentalism are admirable qualities in our society.

We also like people who are smart, clever, or funny. And sometimes clever trumps moral, as our affection for any of the *Ocean's Eleven* movies attests. Show your character outsmarting the opposition or delivering the perfect punch line, and you can have us pulling for someone we might normally find unsavory.

Think about the people you like. Not family or others you're *supposed* to like, but people you can't help liking. Why do you like them? Is it an easygoing manner? A dogged loyalty? A ready laugh? A genuine concern?

Now think about applying one of those attributes to the character you're crafting.

If you're stumped, try to think about what this character's dog likes about him. Dogs like you if you give them the occasional pat and make sure they have something eat. Some cats like you if you just sit still long enough to provide a good warm lap. Don't move on until you've created a character that at least an animal would like!

THE PERCEPTIONS OF OTHERS AND THE DECEPTION OF SELF

We touched on this earlier when we were talking about dress and how successful this character is in achieving the desired look.

The unfortunate truth is that we're not always the best judges of character when it comes to ourselves. The opinions of others make for more reliable, if not altogether charitable, sources of accurate feedback.

By now you should have a good sense of who this character hopes to be and tries to be. She's a wallflower who wants to escape the ghetto of anonymity by dressing loud and speaking boisterously. He's a control freak who is trying to tone himself down to snag a wife.

Unfortunately for our wallflower, she just looks pathetic and weird. Dressed in garish, too-small clothes, painted like a clown, and jabbering on about politics...? It comes off as false and, ultimately, tragic. Others have a much clearer view of her than she has of herself. And I'm sorry to say that our control freak's micromanagement is invisible only to some codependent soul looking for an unhealthy kind of love. Everybody else sees him for the future wife beater that he is.

What about your character? Who does he think he is—and does anyone else agree? He may think he's Apollo in human form, but the ladies see him as the centaur he is. She may feel ugly and useless but others see the beauty of her selfless demeanor.

Most of the time, most characters are pretty close to who they appear to be. A woman is an accountant and she acts like an accountant. A man is a computer geek and he knows it (in fact, he's proud of it and has the Comic-Con shirt to prove it). But even those people can be self-deceived in smaller ways.

"My dad thinks he's a great bowler but I beat him every time."

"Laurie fancies herself this tasteful designer, but have you seen the guest bathroom?"

A self-deceived character is interesting. Blind spots are interesting in fictional characters. They say something important about what this character aspires to be—or hopes not to be.

> A green hunting cap squeezed the top of the fleshy balloon of a head. The green earflaps, full of large ears and uncut hair and the fine bristles that grew in the ears themselves, stuck out on either side like turn signals indicating two directions at once. Full, pursed lips protruded beneath the bushy black moustache and, at their corners, sank into little folds filled with disapproval and potato chip crumbs. In the shadow under the green visor of the cap Ignatius J. Reilly's supercilious blue and yellow eyes looked down upon the other people waiting under the clock at the D. H. Holmes department store, studying the crowd of people for signs of bad taste in dress. Several of the outfits, Ignatius noticed, were new enough and expensive enough to be properly considered offenses against taste and decency. Possession of anything new or expensive only reflected a person's lack of theology and geometry; it could even cast doubts upon one's soul.

> Ignatius himself was dressed comfortably and sensibly.
> The hunting cap prevented head colds. The voluminous
> tweed trousers were durable and permitted unusually free
> locomotion. Their pleats and nooks contained pockets
> of warm, stale air that soothed Ignatius. The plaid flannel
> shirt made a jacket unnecessary while the muffler guarded
> exposed Reilly skin between earflap and collar. The outfit
> was acceptable by any theological and geometrical stan-
> dards, however abstruse, and suggested a rich inner life.
> —**John Kennedy Toole**, *A Confederacy of Dunces*

Green cap, plaid flannel shirt, and a muffler ... and these suggest a rich inner life? Methinks Ignatius's self-awareness may be
a tad askew.

You know what your character thinks about herself. Now
write down how others perceive her. In the clear, frank light of
objectivity, who does this character seem to be?

What others perceive isn't necessarily true. A person who
seems cold might just be shy. And sometimes—often, in fact, if
you're able to take advantage of this in your novel—how someone else perceives a person says as much about the perceiver as
the person being perceived.

But it's still a worthwhile endeavor to examine how this
character comes off to others.

MANNER OF SPEECH

I've intentionally saved this one for last.

Most plot-first novelists rely on a funny way of talking for
the beginning and end of their character-building work.

Ah, he's the Scotsman. And she's the one with the perfect
diction and impressive vocabulary. He's the one who always
says, "Whatever." She's the chick with the lisp.

How are characters differentiated in movies? Easy: They walk on-screen. Instantly the audience perceives that she is not the other girl who was here earlier. She looks different. She's taller. She dresses differently. She's a blonde. But you can't do that in a novel. You can write "Julie entered the room," but that doesn't do anything, by itself, to distinguish Julie from Hannah. You can keep saying, "She toyed with her blond hair" and "The sun glinted off her blond curls" to remind us of what she looks like, but it's never the same as the luxury you have in movies. (Plus, it's annoying to the reader, so don't.)

To differentiate characters in fiction, you have to show them doing and saying things.

So to the plot-first novelist giving a character a funny way of speaking would seem like the perfect solution. I'll make him a Frenchman and let him be the only Frenchman in the book and then everyone will recognize him at the first "Oui, oui!" Or I'll make her talk only about the Dallas Cowboys so she'll start every sentence with "How 'bout them Cowboys?" Perfect! I'm set!

I hope by now you see the shallowness of that approach. A character must be defined by more than one single topic of conversation or by his accent. The Dallas Cowboys girl may love the Cowboys, but she will have other interests or personality quirks as well. Not everyone in France will look, act, and speak exactly like your Frenchman.

I discuss a character's manner and topics of speech last because it is so easily abused.

THE DEUCE YOU SAY!

The way a character speaks can be magical. If you've done your work up to this point, you should be able to craft a character whose identity doesn't even have to be spelled out every time because the reader knows who is speaking.

- "Bond. James Bond."
- "Fasten your seat belts, it's going to be a bumpy night."
- "We thought you was a toad!"
- "I've always relied on the kindness of strangers."
- "Go ahead, make my day."
- "If you only knew how much I loved you. How much I still love you."
- "For it is the doom of men that they forget."[1]

Can you hear those in your head? Do you get an instant gestalt for the characters speaking? Sure, they're movie quotes not novel quotes so maybe it's not a fair test, but the point is that the way a character speaks gives you perfect insight into who he or she is.

> "Fortune is arranging matters for us better than we could have shaped our desires ourselves, for look there, friend Sancho Panza, where thirty or more monstrous giants present themselves, all of whom I mean to engage in battle and slay, and with whose spoils we shall begin to make our fortunes; for this is righteous warfare, and it is God's good service to sweep so evil a breed from off the face of the earth."
>
> "What giants?" said Sancho Panza.
>
> "Those thou seest there," answered his master, "with the long arms, and some have them nearly two leagues long."
>
> "Look, your worship," said Sancho; "what we see there are not giants but windmills, and what seem to be their arms are the sails that turned by the wind make the millstone go."

---

[1] Quotes are from the following films respectively: Any James Bond movie, *All About Eve, O Brother Where Art Thou?, A Streetcar Named Desire, Dirty Harry, Casablanca,* and *Excalibur.*

"It is easy to see," replied Don Quixote, "that thou art not used to this business of adventures; those are giants; and if thou art afraid, away with thee out of this and betake thyself to prayer while I engage them in fierce and unequal combat."

So saying, he gave the spur to his steed Rocinante, heedless of the cries his squire Sancho sent after him.... "Fly not, cowards and vile beings, for a single knight attacks you."

—**Miguel de Cervantes**, *Don Quixote*

You could take out every instance of speech attributions from Sancho and his master and not have a bit of trouble knowing who is speaking. That's the gold standard.

The trick is to grow a character's manner of speech from the inside out. Instead of saying, "He's the Cajun," say, "He's a janitor from a single-parent home with a passion for wounded animals who happens to be from New Orleans." Your character may sound like Forrest Gump, but he will *be* who he really is. The speaking is how his essential character leaks out for the world to see; it is not the sum total *of* his character.

The manner of a character's speech is to fiction what an actor's appearance and costume are to cinema. What we "see her say" in quotation marks must do in a novel what a shot of her doing in a movie will do in film: tone of voice, volume, rate of speaking, vocabulary, inflection, emphasis, pitch. All of these are expressions of who she is on the inside.

And, yes, this includes topics of conversation. She might really talk about the Dallas Cowboys if she loves them. She might even find ways to lead all conversations back to the Cowboys. But that's her as a person having fun and expressing her character. It is not the sum total of her character.

It includes her idioms and colloquialisms. If he's an ophthalmologist he might really say, "We take a dim view of such things" and "I'll keep an eye on it" and "Here's the way I see it," and might not even realize what he's doing. But that's because he has been impacted by his chosen career.

It includes her use—or lack of use—of word pictures or exaggeration or jocularity. These and so many more aspects of what she talks about and how she says it are to be found in her temperament and upbringing.

A person's manner of speech is her marker, her name tag, and her résumé rolled into one.

In 2009 there was a news story about a couple who somehow got past the Secret Service and crashed a State Dinner at the White House though they were not on the guest list. There are now-famous photos of these people shaking hands with President Obama, Vice President Biden, and many more dignitaries. The Secret Service had a terrible time explaining how complete strangers got within striking distance of the leader of the free world—not 200 feet from the Oval Office itself.

These two people were pretenders. They wanted to run with the big dogs. They wanted to be somebodies. But they weren't on the list. They didn't want to do the hard work of actually becoming people who would be invited to a State Dinner with the president. They wanted to cut ahead to the finish line. It's like those people who try to join marathons in the last mile to receive the accolades without doing the work.

Likewise, characters who are nothing more than an accent are pretenders. And the novelists who write them have not yet done the hard work of creating real people. They've tried to cut ahead to the finish line, to sneak into a party they don't belong in, in order to appear as if they've created real characters.

But you're not like that, I know. You're here doing yeoman's work to produce authentic, inside-out characters who speak as they do because that's what comes out when you pair this temperament with this background and realistic parameters. She speaks this way because when you squeeze her, that's what comes out.

ARTICULATE MUCH?

Most novelists are highly intelligent, highly articulate people. They are adept at saying, with precision, exactly what they mean.

That's not to say they always come up with the perfect thing to say in the moment. One of the reasons I'm a writer is that I usually don't come up with the awesome comeback until the moment is over. So I write fiction, during which I think long and hard about the right lines, and then create characters who *do* always say the perfect thing at the perfect time. Revenge!

Perhaps because of this or perhaps even without realizing it, novelists tend to write characters who are as articulate as they are.

That doesn't sound so bad at first. Real life is too full of miscommunication and unclear meanings, so of course we take the opportunity in fiction to bring clarity to our corner of the universe. Fiction isn't about hyper realism as much as it is about verisimilitude, after all. We don't want reality; we want truth.

Realistic dialogue goes something like this:

> "Hey."
> "Hi."
> "How was your … thing? With your review-whatever."
> "Oh, good, I think. She was late."
> "I'm—"
> "And then she was there but … Here's your deodorant."
> "Thanks. I tried to—"

"So she was running late and forgot about— I think she forgot we were ... "
"You're kidding."
"Yeah. So everything was like, 'Hi, you're reviewed, no more leaving early, now get out, I have a lunch.'"
"Oh, that's—"
"I know. But ..." [shrugs]

That may be an accurate transcript, but it's not great dialogue for fiction. Still, you don't want to completely clean it up and clarify it or you'll end up with dialogue that feels "on the nose" and overly polite—and completely unrealistic.

The goal is to hit something in the middle. And you probably won't achieve that with perfectly comprehensible characters saying perfectly logical things all the time.

So how do you write unclear dialogue? It goes against your nature to write something that is intentionally ambiguous, I know. Not all your characters have to be confusing and not every conversation has to go like the one below, but many of your characters will demonstrate some unclear communication at some point in the book.

The roommates we're overhearing below are brushing teeth and getting ready for bed. They've been talking about switching to electric toothbrushes and the like.

Jenny: How long do you have your two?
Laura: My tube? [thinking tube of toothpaste]
Jenny: No, your two.
Laura: My two what?
Jenny: Your two students. [sounding exasperated]
Laura: Oh, I thought you said *tube*. I thought we were still on toothbrushes.
Jenny: No.
Laura: You mean my tutoring students?

Jenny: Yes.

Laura: Oh, they're one hour each.

Jenny: No, how long do you have them?

Laura: [pause] Um, well, one is in the math program, which is twelve weeks, and the other two are in the reading program, which is—

Jenny: No, I mean for two hours.

Laura: [pause] I'm sorry?

Jenny: When one is gone?

Laura: Oh! You mean how long will I have only two students because my third is on vacation?

Jenny: Yes.

Laura: Oh, just Monday and Wednesday. My third student comes back on Friday.

Poor Jenny, bless her. She probably realizes on some level that her communication was unclear, and it may frustrate her more because she doesn't know how to disambiguate it. But to her it all makes perfect sense. In her mind, it was very clear.

Here are some principles of confusing dialogue, should you choose to write some for your characters.

How To Be Confusing

Begin with a non sequitur. Change topics without signaling. They had been talking about toothbrushes, so when Jenny changed to another topic, Laura was still sitting on topic 1.

For best results, use statements that could have meaning with topic 1 but actually pertain to topic 2. Like:

"Yes, that ball game was the best I've seen in a long time."
"When did you see the last one?"
"I actually caught last week's game."
"No, when did you see the last Dalmatian in the park?"
"What?"

To be confusing, mumble so that key words are unclear. "Did you say, 'Do I have a tube?' A tooth? A 'tude?"

As you seek to clarify, use no helper words to give meaning. Simply keep stressing the same word or phrase over and over. "No, a two, a two, a *two!*"

Phrase your sentences so as to have multiple meanings based on context (while concealing context). "How long will you have them?" "Have what?"

Use malapropisms at key points:

> "Will you have to stay in lieu of teaching?"
>> "No, I'll both stay and teach. Is that what you meant?"
>> "But after your teaching, do you also have to stay?"
>> "Oh, you mean in addition to, not in lieu of. In lieu of means instead of."
>> "Are you making fun of me?"
>> "No, I ... what was the question?"

Add a dose of frustration as the other person proves too dense to get what you're saying.

The person being unclear isn't trying to be that way. Indeed, it may cause her great mental angst to realize that she's being unclear and even more angst that she can't find her way out of the maze.

You may try this and find that it becomes too obtrusive for your book. It may turn into a character who is nothing but a comic wrong speaker, like the nurse in *Romeo and Juliet*. Don't let it become a stereotype, of course.

It may be that you try this but decide it doesn't fit for this character or even the whole book. That's fine. Just be conscious about not letting all your characters speak with perfect articulation, like you do. Vary it realistically, based on the other homework you've done for each character's personality.

THE THRESHOLD

Now you are poised. You've crafted what may be the most elaborately understood character you've ever created. Congratulations! You're just about ready to bring this character onstage.

What remains is the inner journey.

To this point you've been equipping your character. You've been training and refining him. You've sent him through boot camp and finishing school. He's outfitted in the best gear. He's been through his psych review so he knows what he'll probably do in a crisis. Now he's ready for the mission.

The mission is his character arc. The next several chapters are going to take this core personality, with this "costume" and background, through a monumental journey of transformation.

Before leaving this chapter, take fifteen minutes to look over what you've done with your character so far. Collate it all. Synthesize. Read over the temperament description with all the rest of what you've dreamed up for her in mind. We'll be doing a full-on character monologue at the end of part 1, but it wouldn't hurt to do a character sketch right now. Write a page describing who this person is. Put it in your own words. Stir the stew.

Now, with that done, we can begin your character's journey to enlightenment.

5

OVERVIEW OF THE
INNER JOURNEY

* * *

THE BEST FICTION IS ABOUT A CHARACTER WHO changes in some significant way.

The selfish brute learns to put others first. The woman marrying for money decides to marry for love. The career ladder climber learns to cut back on his hours to enjoy his family. The bitter old crone learns to let others in. The independent pilot of the *Millennium Falcon* learns to care about a cause. The owner of Rick's Café Americain decides he will stick his neck out for somebody after all.

We love to see characters transformed. Mainly because *we* are being transformed. We know the painful but liberating feeling of ceasing to be one way and beginning to be another, especially if the new way results in more success in relationships or other areas of life we value.

Most of the time, main characters in fiction are changing for the better. It's uplifting to see someone make good choices and improve as a person. Probably your book will be about a character who changes for the best.

But there's room for characters who change for the worse. Indeed, though they may lead to depressing, poor-selling books if given the lead role, these tragic characters are fascinating to watch. Before our very eyes, Roger in *Lord of the Flies,* Allie Fox in *The Mosquito Coast,* and Anakin Skywalker in the *Star Wars* saga all devolve into villains. It's terrible and we want them to stop. But part of us doesn't want them to stop.

Perhaps most intriguing of all is a "bad" character who flirts for awhile with the idea of being good, then decides that his true self is on the dark side of the street. Gollum/Sméagol in *The Lord of the Rings* is a famous example.

Not every story has to be about a character who changes. Certainly we don't expect much change from Indiana Jones. He simply is who he is. There are wonderful stories about characters who don't change at all, whose character is so complete at the beginning of the tale that everyone else must change around her. *Anne of Green Gables* is a terrific example of this. Anne is out of step with everyone. She doesn't fit in. And yet as those around her try to change her to conform, they discover that it is they who are in need of becoming a bit more like Anne. Forrest Gump, WALL-E, Don Quixote, and even Jesus Christ are the agents of change though they themselves do not transform.

But these characters are difficult to write well and suggest a story structure other than what we're doing in this book.

Since we are starting from scratch with your character and book, we're going to create a main character who changes. Whether her ultimate decision is to turn toward or away from the light will be up to you, but we're definitely going to give her a journey in which she is transformed.

THE INNER JOURNEY

In fiction terms, a character's transformation is called his inner journey or character arc. I like the former term as it suggests an odyssey, which it certainly will be for this poor creature you're about to place on stage and commence to torturing.

The heart of this system is your main character's inner journey. Other characters may be on journeys of their own but, for this story at least, it is the protagonist's transformation with which we will be concerned. The core temperament, the birth order, the way others respond to her, her major life events—all of those are *essential* background, but they are background all the same, for the main event, which is her inner journey as it will be explored in your novel.

In *Plot Versus Character* a character's inner journey has five major phases:

- Initial Condition (including the "Knot")
- Inciting Event
- Escalation
- Moment of Truth
- Final State

THE NEXUS

We will discuss each of these phases in the following chapters. But before we begin, it is imperative that you understand that they are steps on a voyage between two points: the "knot" and the moment of truth. I'll explain these terms soon. Just keep in mind that the journey itself is a measure of where the character is along the progression between these two terminal points.

Knot

Moment
of Truth

Everything else is preparation for this quest, progress along this quest, and aftermath of this quest. The simple graph you see right here is the heart of *Plot Versus Character*. It is the thing that is going to ensure that your next novel has both incredible characters and satisfying plot.

THE INNER JOURNEY IN BRIEF

The knot is the thing that is wrong with your character. It's his flaw, his besetting sin, the unhealthy lifestyle he's gotten himself into. It's the harmful thing that the story's whole point is to expose and give him the opportunity to change. I'll give examples in the following chapter, but for now it is enough to know that the knot is the thing that is messing up your character's life.

You as novelist act as Fate or God over this character. You know exactly what's wrong with this person, you see how it's harming him, and you know how to bring it to his attention. You decide you're going to force her to deal with it. You care about her too much to leave her in this handicapped state, so you're going to make her see it and make a decision about it once and for all.

So you begin sending difficulties into her life. She wants to keep things the way they are—stay in an abusive relationship, give up on her dreams, not stand up for herself, hang on to her bitterness, etc.—because, despite the pain of the status quo, it beats the potential pain of change. But you won't let her. So you, as a good fiction deity, rain on her parade. You make it progressively harder for her to ignore the folly of the choices she's making. You bring in positive examples of what her life could be like if she were to try an alternative way. And then you put the squeeze on her (something I like to call Escalation).

It's all about getting her to the point where she will choose, her Moment of Truth. At the outset of the story, she had arrived at an unhappy medium, an imperfect solution that is not good but is at least better than all the other alternatives she's found so far. But through the course of the tale you will show her clearly how her solution is harming her and you will show her the bright, happy land she could enter if she went the new way.

When she gets to this moment of truth, it will be as if she's standing at a crossroads. She needs to be able to perceive what her alternatives are. "I can stay as I am and suffer these real and potential consequences, or I can make this change—at *this* cost—and enjoy these real and potential benefits."

It's that hanging-in-the-balance moment that is the point to which your entire story is heading. You could go so far as to say that this moment is the one and only purpose of the story. What the character chooses in that moment is the all-important thing, the infinite pause when heaven and earth hold their breath to see what this person elects to do in her instant of perfect free choice.

The aftermath of that choice leads to the Final State and the end of the story.

That is your character's inner journey in a nutshell. Part 2 of this book is about the external journey, the stage upon which this person's inner journey is acted out. But make no mistake:

Your book is about what your main character decides at her moment of truth. Everything else is just the vehicle to drive her to that penultimate moment.

Can you see how this is an application of our simple graphic?

Knot   Moment
                                        of Truth

If the destination we're driving to is the moment of truth, then the starting point—the causation point, really—is the knot, the issue causing the problem in the first place. The trip from one to the other is your story. If you build your novel as I recommend, 75 percent of your book will consist of your main character's inner journey.

A WORD ABOUT CHANGE

Up to now, we've been dealing with how a character *is*. We've built a gestalt of everything that has gone into making her who she is.

But from here on, we're going to talk about what the character *can become*. Given this starting point, this temperament, and these layers, how will this character respond when shown she's wrong or dysfunctional in some way and offered a better alternative?

People don't like to change. It's so much easier to stay as we are, even if it's hurting us. "Yes, I know I'm damaging my grade by not turning assignments in on time (or at all), but I'm having too much fun with my party friends to care. Who needs trigonometry, anyway?" In fiction, as in life, people resist change.

Right up until the moment when it hurts too much. People dislike change, but they dislike unacceptable pain and consequences even more. Wait, you mean I could go to jail for that? You mean I won't be able to see my girlfriend anymore—ever? You mean I really am, for sure, 100 percent, going to die if I do this one more time? Dude, what do I need to do to make that not happen?

Your job as story god over this pathetic, *synthetic* human you've created is to bring the pain. You have to dislodge her from her comfortable dysfunction like a pebble you have to remove from a block of mud. The crowbar you use is pain. You have to make it more painful to stay the same than it is to contemplate some manner of character revision. People don't change until it hurts too much to stay the same. Bringing that pain to enable that change ... that's what the inner journey is.

Now that you understand the context, let's discuss the components one by one.

6

THE KNOT

★ ★ ★

"THE MAGISTRATES ARE GOD-FEARING GEN-tlemen, but merciful overmuch—that is a truth," added a third autumnal matron. "At the very least, they should have put the brand of a hot iron on Hester Prynne's forehead. Madame Hester would have winced at that, I warrant me. But she—the naughty baggage—little will she care what they put upon the bodice of her gown! Why, look you, she may cover it with a brooch, or such like heathenish adornment, and so walk the streets as brave as ever!"

"Ah, but," interposed, more softly, a young wife, holding a child by the hand, "let her cover the mark as she will, the pang of it will be always in her heart."

—**Nathaniel Hawthorne,** *The Scarlet Letter*

Your main character needs a problem.

Maybe it's adultery, like our Mistress Prynne. Maybe it's unresolved anger. Maybe it's selfishness (this is a favorite in Disney movies of late, as in *Cars* and *The Game Plan*). Maybe it's a classic tragic flaw like hubris or narcissism or ambition or unwise trusting. Maybe it's a more "modern" sin like drug addiction or pornography or child predation. Perhaps it could be something mundane like discontentment or jealousy or a weakness for chocolate.

It's okay if you haven't thought of one yet. I didn't ask you to. The problem you choose for your character is something anyone could have, so it was important first to establish who this person is, independent of what may afflict her as the story begins. When you have the character's personality firmly set in your mind, it's time to add a problem.

TYING THE KNOT

I refer to your character's problem as his knot. If you've worked with ropes much, especially in a nautical setting, you know they have to run smoothly through eyelets and pulleys and across capstans. A knot in the wrong rope at the wrong place can result in irritation, delay, or even disaster.

So it is with your character. There he is, going along fine, minding his business, when something causes a knot to form in the rope of his life. Maybe he sees it and begins working on untying it. Maybe he sees it and doesn't work on it. Maybe he doesn't see it at all and the problems it's causing are happening in his blind spot.

Whether he knows about it or is working to correct it or not, the knot is messing up his life.

In Mark Spragg's novel *An Unfinished Life*, protagonist Einar is living a solitary life on a ranch. His unresolved grief over the death of his beloved son—and the fuming anger at his daughter-in-law, who was driving the car at the time of the accident—has left him poisoned, bitter, and stunted. Einar doesn't know it. He can't see it. He's stuck in the delicious sadness, if he thinks about it at all. It isn't until he meets a granddaughter he never knew he had that his uneasy truce with life is broken. Old wounds are opened and he is forced to face his crippling anger.

In *Operation: Firebrand,* my protagonist is a Navy SEAL who is involved in a mission that goes wrong. Because of a hesitation during the mission, his best friend is grievously wounded. The story proper begins with him consumed with guilt. He quits the Navy and takes the kind of low-life jobs he feels he deserves. What he's really looking for is a way to kill himself, to end the self-recriminations once and for all. When he is recruited for a new team and a new mission, he believes he's found a way to commit suicide by enemy fire. But he encounters something unexpected that offers him a reason to hope, to live again ... if he will take it.

What knot could you give your character? With the clear sense of who she is as a person (and you might read over your notes to make sure you have that firmly in mind), you can begin thinking about what problem you might want to give her.

HOW TO FIND YOUR KNOT

It's time to have some fun with your character. It's time to put on your Hawaiian shirt and a silly hat and get a little crazy.

When it comes to picking a problem for your hero, the sky's the limit. It's really up to you. Be wacky. Brainstorm. Don't shoot down any idea; just toss 'em all out there.

Do you want her to be afraid of commitment? Addicted to gambling? An out-of-control spender? Go for it. Do you want him to beat his wife? Do you want him to cheat on his taxes? Do you want him to be obsessed with a movie star? Do it.

Here's one guideline: *Go deep.* Play junior psychologist again. Maybe you think it would be fun to have a main character who is scared to go outside. Alex Rover is a character you can appreciate—she's a novelist in Wendy Orr's *Nim's Island*. Alex writes about an Indiana Jones-style adventure hero, but she herself is scared of the mailman, spiders, disease, and just about everything else.

Cool. Good idea. But here's the go-deep question: Why? Why is she scared to go outside? It's not enough to show a symptom like that. You need to know what has caused it.

If you think you'd like to give your character a fixation with ducks, that's okay, but it's not a knot. That's a quirk. You could dig a little deeper and decide that he's obsessed with ducks because his dad was a duck hunter and his one great memory of his dad is a duck-hunting trip. But now his dad has abandoned the family and the character thinks that if he collects the right duck-hunting gear, his dad will come back.

Now we're getting into knot territory. He's feeling sad and angry and adrift and thinking his father left because he wasn't a good enough boy. Aha! When you feel yourself treading into that Freudian, tell-me-about-your-mother land, you know you're getting close to a knot.

Most important: You need to find *something that can carry a full novel.* If your character's knot is that his shirt is untucked and everyone's laughing at him, the solution to which is simply to tuck in his shirt, that's not going to propel a whole story.

That doesn't mean it has to be something earth-shattering, though. The knot doesn't have to be that your hero has a fear of saving the earth but the earth needs saving and somehow he must overcome his fear or the earth is doomed. The fate of the universe doesn't have to hang in the balance. Your knot just has to be significant to the character.

Note that the knot doesn't have to be a fear, though I seem to keep going back to fears because they make for good knots. Other great—and deep-enough—knots are extreme hurt, a lack of forgiveness of someone else, or a lack of forgiveness of self (which we call *guilt*). It can be a deep wound, as when a parent has lost a child to death or abduction. It could be unresolved anguish or a horrible secret. It could be a heavy sense of regret over having done something unwise. It could be awful shame over something done or suffered.

The beauty of it is that it's wide open. So long as it's deep and large enough, it can be anything you wish. Want to explore loyalty between siblings? Give your character the knot of feeling that she's never been loved by her family. Want to investigate the nature of courage—or what it will take to turn a coward into a hero? Then make your character a quailing heart (just be sure you know *why* she prefers flight over fight).

This is really the first time we've begun thinking about story elements. If you're a plot-first novelist you may be feeling pretty good right now. Finally, your comfort zone! If you're a character-first novelist, you might be equally as comfortable because you love thinking about what makes people tick, or change.

If you're feeling a little nervous now, go back to your party hat and crazy shirt: Relax and have fun with it. Dream. Is there a theme you've always wanted to explore? Look in your own life: Is there a loss or fear you'd like to finally grapple with, or an ideal or extreme you'd like to imagine? How about a time when you've failed someone or someone has failed you—want to explore what that must've been like for the other person? Here's your chance to write the ultimate book—the story that finally gives you freedom to tell the tale of your heart.

So the last guideline is *dream big.*

SAMPLE KNOTS

Here are some knots drawn from an array of novels, movies, and real-life experiences:

- The belief that life has dealt him an unfair hand

- A fear of being alone (caused by abandonment as a child)

- A willingness to break any rule to achieve the ultimate approval of her mother

- An overpowering desire to exact revenge

- A fear of commitment (caused by parents' divorce)

- A hoarding of clothes and food (caused by living through the Great Depression)

- An unwillingness to let a child have fun (because she lost another child through indulgence)

- A willingness to endure continued abuse (because his parents were abusive and that's the only way he understands love)

- A loner mentality (caused by being hurt by someone she relied upon)

- A belief that he is worthless and a resulting self-sabotage to make his reality line up with his belief

Get the idea? You want to wound your character in some way or give her a tragic flaw or "besetting sin" that causes her life to be less than it should be.

It might even help to think of it in medical terms. The patient has a tumor. She doesn't know it yet—or maybe she does but doesn't want to deal with it—but it's killing her all the same. You as her surgeon want to get it out quick, but she keeps missing her appointments with you. You can see how it's hurting her and how it will hurt her if left untreated.

What kind of wringer do you want to put your poor character through? What kind of tumor do you want to give him?

CONSIDER THE ALTERNATIVE

As you're thinking about the particular kind of misery you're going to sic on your main character, also be thinking about what Door #2 should look like.

Let's say you're thinking you'd like to make your protagonist scared to be around children because when she was young she dropped her baby brother and he's been a vegetable ever since. She is beset with guilt, though she goes to see him every weekend. She won't hold anyone's baby, ever. But the guilt has exceeded normal bounds. She intentionally has deprived herself of any good thing in her life. She didn't go to veterinary school, as she'd always dreamed, because that would've meant moving away from her brother. She hasn't dated, much less married, because she feels she doesn't deserve such joys in her life if her brother will never get to have them.

Pretty interesting character, actually. You can just see her wearing ratty clothes and frumpy hair and maybe she's even intentionally unhygienic so as to dissuade any would-be suitors. It's definitely a knot that is big enough to propel an entire novel.

Now it's time to imagine what the alternative could be. If you are Fate in this story and you're not going to let her remain in her miserable stew, what are you going to try to get her to change to? What is the happy other possibility you'd like her to see and possibly seize?

Maybe you'd like to see her forgive herself and finally give herself permission to have a life. That's a radically different existence than what she's currently embracing. It would take a lot of convincing for her to let go of the self-loathing she has such a death grip on. But it would make for an interesting novel! Already you can begin thinking of ways you might bring that optimistic possibility into her life. That's what you're looking for.

In *An Unfinished Life,* Einar begrudgingly allows his daughter-in-law and granddaughter into his world. The more they hang around, the more he glimpses what it would feel like to love again, to care again, to invest again into a young person's life. The crypt of his soul is pierced by a shaft of light, and for a moment it feels good. For a moment he is almost tempted to let go of all this cancerous anger and become the kind of man he was before he lost his son.

As you're looking for a good alternative to your hero's problem, *make sure it's the opposite of her knot.* It's great that you present a happy option of your hero getting promoted to organizer of the homecoming parade, but if that promotion isn't the antithesis of her knot, it will have no impact. It would work great if she sees herself as a nobody who is capable of nothing good. But if her knot is that she feels abandoned, the parade job won't be therapeutic to her in any way. It will just feel like more work.

So what will it be for your main character? Given the following knot, what would be the most attractive substitute outcome? If he's addicted to online role-playing games (and you'd of course want to delve into the *why* behind his addiction), what would be the best alternative in his eyes? Maybe it's the ability to go through a day free of the tyranny of those games; the ability to make his own choices and spend his days—and his money—as he pleases.

GETTING THERE

Getting to that happy destination will not be easy. One doesn't lightly walk away from addictions or negative strongholds. Your character has become comfortable in her dysfunction. Forget our crowbar—it will take something akin to a nuclear blast to get her to leave it.

Ah, fiction. It's good to be a god.

Find a great knot for your main character. Then find an equally powerful promised land to offer in exchange. The bulk of his inner journey—and of your book itself—is going to be the interplay (more like *battle*) between these two options—all leading up to that breathless moment when he decides once and for all which door he's going to step through.

7

THE MOMENT OF TRUTH

* * *

THE LIGHT SPRANG UP AGAIN, AND THERE on the brink of the chasm, at the very Crack of Doom, stood Frodo, black against the glare, tense, erect, but still as if he had been turned to stone.

"Master!" cried Sam.

Then Frodo stirred and spoke with a clear voice, indeed with a voice clearer and more powerful than Sam had ever heard him use, and it rose above the throb and turmoil of Mount Doom, ringing in the roof and walls.

"I have come," he said. "But I do not choose now to do what I came to do. I will not do this deed. The Ring is mine!" And suddenly, as he set it on his finger, he vanished from Sam's sight.

—**J.R.R. Tolkien**, *The Lord of the Rings*

This is the climactic moment. Frodo and Sam have traveled together for endless miles and endured tragedy and peril to get them to this place, the inside of a volcano, the only place where the treacherous Ring of Power may be destroyed. Frodo need only drop it into the lava below and the deed will be done and all free peoples saved.

Tolkien has done a marvelous job of bringing the main character's inner journey to its pinnacle at the same moment that the external story is at its apex, thus doubling the tension. Literally, the fate of the world hangs on what one character *decides* to do.

And that, dear writer friend, is what we're going to do with your novel.

WE'RE AT THE END ALREADY?

It feels strange to be talking about the end of your main character's journey—and of the book itself—before we're halfway into this book, I know. We haven't even talked about the beginning of the journey, so how can we be talking about the climactic moment?

I have found that talking about things out of order can sometimes be an aid to understanding. By considering the point you are trying to reach, you can then work backwards to figure out the steps you need to take to get there.

Let's go back to our simple graphic:

Knot   Moment of Truth

The power of your story will be the strength of this central dyad. In a way, your entire story is just a vehicle to transport the reader to the moment of truth. *The Lord of the Rings* was about many things, but the crucial bit, the part when moons and stars paused in their orbits (literally speaking), was the passage quoted above: Frodo's moment of truth. In a broad sense, everything else in the entire epic was simply setup for that moment.

In the previous chapter you picked your main character's knot, the "sin" that the story god has decided to purge him of. All the events of the story are the tools Fate is using to cause her to get to the moment of truth. Figuring out where your hero's character arc is headed will enable us to find the whole structure of the story.

You don't have to decide now which path the character is going to take at the moment of truth, by the way. For now, it's all about getting her there.

WHAT IS THE MOMENT OF TRUTH?

Simply put, the moment of truth is when your character makes her decision.

She's been going down Path A for a long time. She would still be happily (or miserably) going down that path if the events of the story hadn't come along. Now there's that pesky Path B to consider. "Man, it looks pretty good. It would sure solve a lot of problems if I went that way. It comes at a price, though. Am I willing to pay? Ooh, I hate decisions."

Throughout the course of the story she's been making minor choices, little moments of truth. For months, Frodo has been dealing with the temptation to use or even keep the ring for himself. Each time, he avoids the temptation. And even when he doesn't, he regrets it and recommits to his original purpose to destroy it. Those have been play-off games leading to the Super Bowl, so to speak. Each has been important, and if he had chosen poorly before, he wouldn't have gotten to the big game, but in the end it's all been lead-up to the main event.

So it will be with your character. Because you know the old way, the way of the knot, and the new way that leads to the promised land, you will be able to bring both into play in escalating intensity as the story goes along. Both sides will have their say. Reps from both companies will have their turn to tout their wares. Evangelists from both sides will get their turn in the pulpit. And like an undecided shopper at a middle-eastern bazaar, called this way and that by earnest criers, your hero will be tempted.

At each juncture, your main character learns more and more what is at stake. He begins to glimpse just how poisonous his current way is—and just how wonderful the other way might be, if it truly is as advertised. He comes to understand both the promise and the price of the two ways. He comes, in other words, to truly understand his choice.

It is at that moment, when his last reason for staying the same has been knocked away and he must choose once and for all, that you are heading toward. It's the reason you are writing your novel.

That is your book's moment of truth.

Your hero is standing at the crossroads. No, let's make it more picturesque. Your hero is balancing on the end of a girder one hundred stories above the pavement. She can't go backward because … because an alien creature is coming toward her down the girder. If she stays as she is, cold and alone and clinging to balance, the creature will consume her—or worse. But that *is* one of her options. Her other option is to try to leap to a rooftop across and below. If she takes a running start, she can probably make it. Firefighters have set up a fall pad for her and are standing by to administer first aid.

Whatever she's going to do or not do, it has to be now.

This is the moment of truth.

FAMOUS MOMENTS

We've already looked at the moment of truth from *The Lord of the Rings*. Let's see some others to help illustrate what I'm talking about.

- Romeo's moment comes when he's in the tomb beside his (supposedly) dead Juliet. Now that he believes he's in the world without her, what will he do?

- Darth Vader's moment of truth comes in *Return of the Jedi* when the Emperor is killing Luke Skywalker: Will the evil Emperor win his ultimate allegiance or will Vader betray his dark master to save his son?

- Elizabeth's moment of truth in *Pride and Prejudice* comes when she realizes Mr. Darcy, whom she has snubbed, has actually saved her family from great shame. Suddenly he's not what she thought he was, and he's asking her to marry him—what is she going to do?

- In *Pirates of the Caribbean: Dead Man's Chest,* Captain Jack Sparrow is in a rowboat paddling away to safety, leaving his crew and friends to die. He puts his oars down, turns back to look, and ... has his moment of truth.

- In *Of Mice and Men* George's moment comes when he's alone with Lennie after Lennie has killed Curley's wife. If George—who has a gun—lets Lennie go, the lynch mob will get him. Yet he knows Lennie can't be allowed to be free anymore. What will he do?

- Captain Ahab's moment of truth comes when Starbuck tells him that the chase for Moby Dick is blasphemous and people are dying. Will Ahab see reason or pursue the whale to the doom of himself and his entire crew?

Do you see how the author brings the main character to the brink? The hero fully understands what will probably happen if he goes through Door #1 and what will probably happen if he goes through Door #2. The choices are clearly laid out before him. He understands the risk and consequences. Then he chooses, and the impact of the choice plays out from there.

That is the moment of truth.

THE CONTENDERS

If your hero's knot is a bitterness that has left her sad and lonely, perhaps the alternative you pick for her is to release her anger, forgive the person who wronged her, and rejoin the human race. So if you locked those two options in a room together and let them fight it out, what would happen?

Maybe at first the pleasant alternative just looks like foolishness to her. Maybe you personify it by having a special needs child move in next door. The child is always happy despite his many handicaps. *Silly, stupid child,* she thinks. But of course you have the child insinuate his way into her life. Subtly at first, and then with more vigor, she tries to get him to face his impediments and get angry about it. But his positive outlook proves indefatigable. She smiles at him in spite of herself. She begins to appreciate his visits, to hear in her head his outlook on things.

Finally you bring the journey to a crossroads. The woman is faced with a major decision. For the first time in a long time she can imagine herself making a positive choice. It would mean giving up her hatred. It would mean taking a chance to trust someone else and possibly be hurt. But it would get her something she longs for, perhaps a reconnection with the boy, since he has now stopped coming over.

And so she has a choice to make: Stay with the old way (and enjoy its safety but endure its continued toxins) or go with the new way (and risk failure or ridicule but have a chance at joy).

Okay, that's a hypothetical example. Let's look at *The Lord of the Rings.* The story gives several characters their moments of truth, all regarding the One Ring. It's almost a study in the variety of reactions to the ring, a litmus test for character quality. Gandalf has his chance at the ring, as do Farimir, Borimir, Aragorn, Sam, Gollum, Bilbo, Galadriel, Saruman, and more.

But the main one is Frodo. He carries it for the bulk of the trilogy. His knot is to use the power of the ring to serve his own interests. The cost of doing that would be the destruction of all he holds dear—even as he seeks to save it—and the loss of his own soul to the corrupting power of the ring. He knows this, but still the siren song is appealing. The alternative, the "right thing" to do, is to deny himself the temptation of the ring and instead bring about its destruction.

It's a great conflict woven into the fabric of the story. (We're going to give your story one of these too.) You can see that at every step he would be torn in opposing directions. To have the means of your salvation as near as your hand and yet refuse to use it, even when in danger or when friends are in danger, to serve a larger but more distant good ... hoo boy. Not sure I could be as strong as our surprising little hobbit.

During the story, the two desires vie for Frodo's loyalty. The Black Riders are sending out psychic signals, urging the Ring-bearer to put it on and use its power—because by doing so he reveals his location to them. The ring itself longs to be found and taken back to its evil master. Situations come in which it is almost impossible *not* to use the ring's invisibility to get free of danger. And yet on the other side are Gandalf and Aragorn and Galadriel and others urging him to never use it, for the safety of his own soul (not to mention everyone else's life). It is a powerful internal conflict and it propels both Frodo's inner journey and the reader all the way through the story.

The goal of the novelist is to bring these two choices, these two options, together in an ultimate moment of choosing for the main character. We've seen how Tolkien did it. There stands Frodo at the edge of the Cracks of Doom, having surmounted incredible obstacles to arrive here at the place of the ring's potential destruction, facing the final choice at last. Compounding the tension is that his friends are at that very moment fighting for their lives on a battlefield not far away, a battle whose outcome rests on what he does with the ring inside Mount Doom.

In *Star Wars* (Episode IV), you could build a case that Luke Skywalker's knot is a faith in technology and what man and science can do. His happy alternative is to put his faith in the Force, a more spiritual solution, which—if true—supersedes the abilities both man and science can bring to bear. Luke experiences his moment of truth as he's speeding through the trench on the surface of the Death Star, with bad guys all around him and good guys dropping like flies, with the good guys' secret base almost within range of the Death Star's weapons.

He turns on his targeting computer, which denotes his reliance on technology. The goal is to shoot an energy weapon (a proton torpedo) into a very small portal at the end of this trench. Everyone else in his position would try to use the targeting computer to guide the missile into the hole. That's the way he's leaning too. Except that he's been getting a taste of the power of the Force throughout the film. This spiritual thing that promises to be better even than technology. Plus he has the voice of his mentor in his head telling him to trust the Force.

With the fate of the free galaxy in the balance, Luke has a choice to make. It's his moment of truth.

PICKING THE MOMENT OF TRUTH FOR YOUR CHARACTER

To find the moment of truth for your main character, bring to mind your hero's knot. You've got her "problem" already figured out. You've also chosen the alternative, the sunny land of promise she could get to if she lets go of the old way and embraces the new way. With this dialectic in hand, you're ready to figure out your hero's moment of truth.

Here are some things to keep in mind as you craft this all-important moment:

- *Make it fit*—It (almost) goes without saying that the moment of truth has to be the collision of the two contenders in the hero's life. You've got the old way and the new way. In your character's moment of truth, she decides between those two options.

- *Make sure both options are compelling*—Your hero is stuck in the old way, which is hurting him on some level, and yet it gives him something he values. The new way has to be at least as attractive to him as the old way, even if he doesn't see it at first. It must give him everything the old way is not giving him, and it must solve problems for him—but not without cost.

- *Include the cost of purchase*—The moment of truth is not complete unless the hero understands not only what he stands to gain by choosing one option over the other, but also what he stands to lose. If he lets go of his self-loathing to embrace a positive view about himself, it will be a betrayal of his father, who always said he was worthless. If she lets go of her fear and moves on with her life, it will mean risking failure again.

- *Provide smaller moments of truth along the way*—We'll discuss this fully in the chapter on the escalation, but for now just keep in mind that you will need to think of ways for these two opposing options to skirmish before the decisive battle. Just as Frodo had temptations to use the ring at multiple junctures in the story (and in some of these, he chose *wrong*) and as Luke saw the promise of the Force over the limits of technology, your character will need to make minor yes/no choices between these two options before the big moment of truth.

Now it's time to choose the moment of truth for your book. Fill in these blanks for your main character:

- My main character's knot is _____.

- This handicaps him/her in this way:_____
  _____.

- My main character has chosen or allowed this state of affairs because it gives him/her this benefit:_____
  _____.

- The happy alternative (the "new way") I'm going to set before my main character is: _____
  _____.

- It's a perfect foil or counterbalance to the old way because
  _____.

- The new way will provide these benefits to my main character: _____.

- But my main character will not initially consider this new way to be a real option for him/her because_____
  _____.

- After awhile, though, my main character begins to see that he/she would probably enjoy the following benefits if he/she went with the new way: _____

  _____.

- The cost of going this new way will also become clear to my main character over time. He/She will come to see that if she does this, she will have to _____

  _____. It's a price he/she is not entirely sure he/she is willing to pay.

PULLING IT ALL TOGETHER

With all these ingredients bubbling in the stew, you're ready to add the final element.

The question is, why now? Why does your character have to make this choice right now? In our steel girder example, there was an alien monster barreling down on our hero, so she had to make a choice in a hurry. What will it be in your character's life that is forcing her to choose without further delay? It's up to you to force this choice. It's what everything has been pointing to from page 1.

I'm not saying you have to know your plot as of yet. You may not have a clue whether your book is going to be more like *Jaws* or *Gone with the Wind*. That's fine. What we're looking for is the corner you're going to back your hero into—metaphorically speaking—that forces her to choose now.

You'll find your "why now?" component in the nature of the two contenders themselves. If the knot is an overdependence on technology and the alternative is a reliance on something spiritual, your moment of truth will have to be something that forces the character to choose between those two options. Sounds obvious, I know, but it's important to say it clearly. And your "why now?" will be some factor that puts a time limit on the decision.

If the knot is a bitterness that has left the hero isolated and lonely and the alternative is letting go of the anger to forgive and embrace what's left of his family (*An Unfinished Life*), the moment of truth will be something that makes him jump off the fence one way or another. Maybe the granddaughter is going to leave if he doesn't reach out to her. The moment of truth becomes what he's going to decide to do—hold on to the old way and be miserable or let go of his delicious anger to embrace the new way—and the "why now?" element is what's making him have to finally take action without further delay. Act now or forever regret it.

Often the moment of truth will come when the hero's last resistance has been knocked away. He's hit rock bottom and he realizes the depravity of his old way. It has finally cost him too much. His eyes have been opened at last, and now he's able to make a sober choice.

As we've seen, characters don't change until it hurts too much to stay the same. A woman may not be willing to leave her family homestead, despite the rising floodwaters. But when the water comes in and her infant daughter is almost swept away, suddenly Granny's old quilts don't seem so important.

So bring on the pain. Be willing to throw lightning bolts at your character, zapping away his arguments, until he can finally compare both options and evaluate them as equals, as real, valid choices *for him.*

What will be your main character's moment of truth? You can always adjust it later, but what are you thinking right now?

To quote Master Yoda, "Upon this, all depends."

8

INITIAL CONDITION

$\star \ \star \ \star$

WHETHER I SHALL TURN OUT TO BE THE
hero of my own life, or whether that station will be held
by anybody else, these pages must show.
——**Charles Dickens,** *David Copperfield*

Pretend you're a doctor seeing a new patient. You're a family practitioner, so you're often the first interface a person has with the medical world. Your patient complains of an ongoing pain in her shoulder. She thinks it's a muscle strain and wants pain medication. You suspect it's something normal like that, but the fact that it's been going on for years makes you wonder.

So you do an exam. Yes, there is pain, especially when she holds the arm in certain positions. You probe and press, but it's inconclusive. It could be nothing but it could be something. You order tests.

At the beginning of your novel, your main character has an undiagnosed ailment. Maybe he feels the pain of it enough to seek out professional help, but probably not. If he feels the pain at all, he's got his own ways of self-medicating. No need bothering anyone else about it—or admitting it.

Or maybe he's like the man I heard about who happened to be introduced to a doctor at a restaurant. When they shook hands, the doctor noticed an extreme weakness in the other man's grip. He suggested the man go in for tests, and the tests revealed a serious condition that was remedied through aggressive intervention. But the man didn't even know he had a problem.

Because you've taken your character through *Plot Versus Character* this far, you know exactly what his problem is. You're like the radiologist who has read the MRI and are just waiting to drop the bomb on the patient. Poor slob, he has no idea what's in his future.

Here's our graphic again:

The knot is his problem and the whole story is a vehicle transporting him to his moment of truth. We know what these two points look like now. With that foundation firmly laid, we can begin building upon it.

Here's a glimpse at the full journey schematic:

You can still see our knot and moment of truth dyad, but now it's been built out with the rest of the inner journey structure.

Briefly, the *initial condition* is how our story finds the main character. In that early portion, we'll encounter the character's *knot* or problem. The *inciting event* is the wrench thrown into the gears, the detour that sends her on this journey in the first place. The *escalation* is the intensifying struggle between the old way and the new way, all leading to the *moment of truth*. What she decides in her moment of truth determines her *final state*, how she is at the end of the story.

ONCE UPON A TIME ...

At the end of this chapter we'll create a monologue that captures the essence of your main character, including her knot. This can be used as the basis for the scene when you bring her onstage the first time (which we'll talk about in part 2).

At this point we're thinking like a physician: How is her as-yet-undiagnosed ailment affecting her? How is your main character's knot messing with her life as the story begins?

Start with your camera lens zoomed way out and then slowly zoom in. If a person (any person) were to have the knot you've chosen for this character, how might it affect him or her? Brainstorm a hundred different ways a person might deal with it. Come up with a page or more of logical conclusions that a person so afflicted might end up at.

Let's say your main character has a fear of abandonment. Before considering how *this* character would compensate for a fear of abandonment, just create the pool of all possible reactions any-one might come up with. Don't be afraid to be a little nutty here.

She's afraid of abandonment so she has chained herself to her best friend. She has prostituted herself (literally or figura-tively) to do whatever her boyfriend desires so he won't leave her. She has hardwired Facebook and Twitter into her cerebral cortex so she'll always feel connected to her peeps. She lives in a YMCA encampment. She has six roommates. She has thirteen cats. She makes all potential friends and boyfriends sign legally binding documents promising to never leave or forsake her, on penalty of the forfeiture of a portion of their assets. She married early and has nine kids. She's on every committee and in every club in town. She does her best thinking at the play area at a shopping mall on December 24th. She's kidnapped six people and keeps them in the basement … just to talk.

Okay, so I've gotten a little crazy as I've thought up many possible ways of dealing with a fear of abandonment, as I'm sure you have too. Now your job is to apply these ideas to this particular character. You've done your homework so you know why this fear arose. Keep that in mind because her compensatory behaviors will be perfectly suited to numb that exact kind of pain. Now bring in your understanding of this character's temperament and all the other layers, and extrapolate from there. How would *this* character with *this* background try to avoid experiencing the pain of her knot?

It might help to go big at first. Go to the nth degree. Imagine what it would look like if your hero were to go off the deep end. Then scale it back from there.

If his knot is a distrust of people, the ultimate compensation would be to live in a shack on the top of a mountain. Surrounded by an electrified fence. With lots of dogs. Because he's not lost his connection with reality, he hasn't moved to Tibet just yet. But you should be able to see elements of it in his daily life. If the nth degree would be on the level of psychosis, what would it look like if it were only at the level of mild neurosis?

Maybe he has one dog, but it used to be a police dog. Maybe he owns a top-of-the-line security system. Maybe he regularly hires a private detective to do background checks on people he meets and might possibly develop a relationship with. Maybe he reads spy handbooks and employs motion-controlled cameras and doubles back on his route to be sure no one is following.

You could imagine how he might act in interpersonal relationships. Half-joking comments about secretly coming over to your house to surveil you. Always sitting with his back to the wall in public places. A history of ending perfectly good relationships out of the blue—doing unto others before they can do unto him.

At the beginning of Jim Stovall's novel *The Ultimate Gift* Jason Stevens is the spoiled grandson of a deceased billionaire. Mark Spragg's *An Unfinished Life* begins with Einar alone and bitter. Katniss is certain she will die, at the beginning of *Hunger Games* by Suzanne Collins, but by the end she is confident in her skills. Bilbo shuns every adventure and is content with his humdrum life at the beginning of J.R.R. Tolkien's *The Hobbit*. At the beginning of Jane Austen's *Emma,* Emma fancies herself a brilliant matchmaker and spectacular human being, but she is destined to learn otherwise.

Night at the Museum begins with Larry divorced, unemployed, and chasing another useless scheme. *Never Been Kissed* begins with Josie afraid and full of angst. *Spider-Man* begins with Peter as a lowly dweeb too shy to ask Mary Jane out.

If you'll excuse the crass example, your character must start out constipated. Severely impacted. And suffering the related pain and discomfort. She's constitutionally stuck. It is the purpose of the story to get her unstuck.

ALL KNOTTED UP

What about your character? How is his knot affecting him when the story begins?

You want it to be hindering him but probably not paralyzing him. Mary Poppins enters into a dysfunctional family, with Mr. Banks being the most constipated of them all. Yet they are all muddling through their lives unaware that there's anything wrong. It isn't until the incorrigible Mary Poppins brings all manner of mayhem into the Banks' household—and even causes Mr. Banks to lose his job—that they can throw off their malaise and enjoy emotional health.

So it is with your character. She's making it through life fairly well. She is frustrated by a few things, but she's certain her plan will ease that frustration if she can just get X to happen.

Allow the knot to hurt her, but don't let it consume her. Not yet. She is more than her problem, after all. She is not Alcoholic-Woman or Fear-Woman. She is a fully realized character, with a temperament and talents and history and appearance and zeal … who also happens to have come down with a bad case of "the knot."

Your hero has to be likable at the beginning of your story, as I've mentioned. He can't be too far gone. He can't be psychotic, at least not at the outset. The potential for craziness will be there, of course. Indeed, it will be your job as story god to drive him to the brink. But he can't start out there. We have to like him first.

With all that in mind, write down how your main character's knot is affecting him as the curtain rises.

If you've already done this for your protagonist and you're going back through for another major character, the question might not be how his knot is impacting him at the beginning of the book, but how it's impacting him just before the first time we meet him.

SOLILOQUY

Now that you've envisioned how your main character's knot is affecting him at the beginning of the story, your character development homework is complete.

We still have three more chapters on her inner journey, but in terms of who this person is and how the story finds her, our work is done.

Now it's time to synthesize. To collate. To toss it all in the blender and hit puree.

The final phase in understanding your character's personality is to write a monologue in which he steps onstage in the penultimate way, doing a perfectly typical thing, caught in the ideal surroundings, revealing the essence of who he is. It's a metaphysical gazetteer into his soul just at the moment when he reveals in a nutshell who he is.

We could've written this at the end of chapter 4, when we knew all about who she is and how she got to be that way. You may actually want to write a synthesizing monologue for that moment because it will capture all the ingredients of who she is *independent of any story considerations or knots.* You could refer back to that scene from book to book as the same character continues in your series. It would be as if you've bottled her essence and could always take it off the rack and sample it again to remind you of who she is. Like a snapshot or, to use my more speculative animation, a clone frozen in suspended animation.

If you do that in chapter 4, just be sure you also do a new (or at least appended) monologue for this character whenever you are about to place him in a story. It's good to know who this character is in isolation, carved in marble and untouched by trouble or time. But when it's time to write a novel, you need to know how that person is when afflicted by an undiagnosed tumor.

SET THE STAGE

Let's set the ultimate stage for your character to make her entrance. Think of this as a dream or vision in which the soul of this person appears in her ideal surroundings.

Where is he? If he could pick any place to be—based on his temperament, background, and knot—where would it be? Beside a creek on an old log by a campfire? In the Oval Office? Curled up in an overstuffed chair by the hearth? Hurtling over category VI rapids in an airalite kayak? In the boardroom at the head of a mahogany conference table? On a throne? Spaceship? Archaeological dig?

Where would he be if he could pick the ultimate place to be found? If he knew he were going to be painted by a famous portrait artist, what setting would he choose? A character-capturing sculpture for *Lost*'s John Locke might portray him standing at the hatch, ready to open it. A character who is a soldier forever in his heart might be portrayed leaning against a partially destroyed desert stone wall, watching for the enemy.

Then choose the costume. What would she be wearing? A macabre way of getting at what I'm trying to get at here is to ask what she'd like to be buried in—and where she'd like to be buried. What is her favorite outfit, the one that most makes her feel like herself? Grungy old overalls for rutting around in the garden? Strapless evening gown? Jeans and an oversize sweatshirt? Her dress blues or combat fatigues? Bikini? Wedding dress? Surgical gown? If she could pick the outfit that most typified her, what would it be?

What about props and actions? What would she be doing? That man sitting on the log by the campfire, is he whittling a block of wood? Cleaning a fish? Roasting s'mores? That woman curled up in the overstuffed chair, can you see her wrapped in her favorite Afghan, cradling a good novel and a steaming mug of Italian blend espresso? Or an itty-bitty dog? Or a laptop?

Now that you know where he is and what he's wearing, think about what he'd be doing. This is more important than where he'd be and what he'd be wearing rolled together. Your choice of action to capture his personality perfectly is crucial. Take a long, slow read back through all your notes. Concentrate on temperament and major elements of his background.

Factor in her knot. But don't overdo it. She shouldn't be doing something that is completely caused by her knot. If her knot is that she's afraid of open places because of a tornado that took her family, in this scene she shouldn't be living in a cavern 200 feet underground. Unless you really do want to show her as a psycho, back off a bit on the knot. Lean more toward who she is permanently, not how she's temporarily acting because of her problem. Yet in something she does or talks about during this scene you're about to write, reveal how the knot is affecting her, even if she doesn't see it herself.

WHAT TO TALK ABOUT?

In this altered consciousness moment, when you get an uncanny look directly into this character's soul, what would he talk about? It's soliloquy time.

What you're aiming for is a free-flowing revelation of her personality. Have her come onstage doing a typical action and talking about the topic nearest and dearest to her heart.

Seek to capture her manner of *thinking* as much as her manner of speaking. Go back through your notes looking for those factors that would determine her speech. Did she grow up in Manhattan or the hills of Kentucky? Does she speak like the articulate individual she is or like she ain't got no schoolin'? Does she use word pictures or are such things frivolous? Do terms from her career spice up her terminology?

This soliloquy is your graduation project. You've gone through all the work to learn who this character is, and now it's time for your thesis. That's what you're creating with this monologue. It's the synthesis of everything you know about her.

Give it your best, and don't move on until you know you've nailed it. Keep writing the scene until you can hear this character's voice clearly in your head—and not only his topics and manner of speech but his way of thinking. What you're doing is creating his *voice*. You're after a particular, distinctive verbalization construct that perfectly conveys how he views the world and how his mind works.

In cinema, the camera reveals a character's appearance and posture and dress and everything else at a glance. But in fiction, you don't have that luxury. In fiction, you have to rely on how the person speaks to remind the reader of who he is in his essence. When you've created a character voice that is this rich and distinctive, you can get away with dropping dozens of speech attributions in your book. When the person speaks in such a way as to typify her, the "Milicent said" bits are superfluous. That's what you're going for: characters who differentiate themselves simply by opening their mouths.

Consider how the speaker's character is revealed in the following excerpts:

> If you really want to hear about it, the first thing you'll probably want to know is where I was born, and what my lousy childhood was like, and how my parents were occupied and all before they had me, and all that David Copperfield kind of crap, but I don't feel like going into it, if you want to know the truth.
>
> —J.D. Salinger, *The Catcher in the Rye*

> I wish either my father or my mother, or indeed both of them, as they were in duty both equally bound to it, had minded what they were about when they begot me; had they duly considered how much depended upon what they were then doing;—that not only the production of a rational Being was

concerned in it, but that possibly the happy formation and temperature of his body, perhaps his genius and the very cast of his mind;—and, for aught they knew to the contrary, even the fortunes of his whole house might take their turn from the humours and dispositions which were then uppermost:—Had they duly weighed and considered all this, and proceeded accordingly,—I am verily persuaded I should have made a quite different figure in the world, from that, in which the reader is likely to see me.

—**Laurence Sterne,** *The Life and Opinions of*
Tristram Shandy, Gentleman

It is hard to describe, this buzzing in my head. It wakes me, obviously. But it is hard to clarify for someone like you—at least the type of person I assume you to be—someone with a free head. We haven't had true freeheads since before the date change, and that's really before I remember. Before I'm allowed to remember. I'll just try to be lucid, though, in hopes you can follow along.

Anyway, the vibration wakes me from chute sleep, meaning someone needs a debugger. It rarely happens anymore, but it happens. So early in the day. Crichton, I hate early. I blame that on the buzzer itself, but I could be wrong there. I mean, you'd think they'd want me to sleep. Otherwise, how can I perform?

—**Kerry Nietz,** *A Star Curiously Singing*

I, Tiberius Claudius Drusus Nero Germanicus This-that-and-the-other (for I shall not trouble you yet with all my titles) who was once, and not so long ago either, known to my friends and relatives and associates as "Claudius the Idiot," or "That Claudius," or "Claudius the Stammerer," or "Clau-Clau-Claudius" or at best as "Poor Uncle Claudius," am now about to write this strange history of my life; starting from my earliest childhood and continuing year by year until I reach the fateful point of change where, some eight years ago, at the age of fifty-one, I suddenly found myself caught in what I may call the "golden predicament" from which I have never since become disentangled.

—**Robert Graves**, *I, Claudius*

WRITER, WRITE

It's time. Write the scene.

Set the stage. Bring your character on. Describe what he's wearing and doing. Then begin the monologue. Put it in first person (I/me/my)—unless he's a king speaking in the imperial plural or a schizophrenic speaking for the crowd inside him.

Keep going for one page. Seven pages. Twenty pages. As long as it takes to round the corner on her voice. The very act of writing in a character voice may be new to you, so don't cut it short if you're enjoying it. You may need to come back occasionally as you're writing the book and write an extension to the scene, just to get you back in that body and mind-set again.

This scene is the "character Bible" for this character. It is the culmination of all the work you've done in building this distinctive personality. Refer to it often.

Remember to include a hint of his knot somewhere in the monologue. Just have him steer his self-revelatory rambling over in that direction for a while, then move on. Indicate his level of awareness of its presence. Show why he's in this situation; why he doesn't change even though it's uncomfortable. Have him spill his guts. Then move on to other aspects of his personality.

When you feel you have his character in your head, have him describe a room or a traffic accident or a person. Bring on a parade of things for him to respond to, to be sure you have a feel for how he'd interpret things as they happen.

Finally, bring another person onstage with him. See how he interacts. You need to know this. Maybe bring on a series of individuals or even small groups for him to relate to. You need to be able to keep your hold on his voice even when other voices and personalities are present.

When you've gone through this complete character-building exercise more than once, try writing scenes with two or more of these people onstage together. Write the same scene over again for each character, telling it from his or her perspective, changing voices like pairs of shoes. When you can do that and keep them all straight, you will have earned your merit badge.

HURRAY!

Congratulations for creating what may be your very first distinctive, not-you character. It is a cause for celebration.

You may find yourself using this scene you've just written for more than character development. In part 2 we're going to talk about the early scene in your novel in which you bring your main character onstage for the first time. It needs to be a scene that reveals the essence of her character. You will be wise to come back to this scene, the one you've just written, at that time. You will find in it a wonderful basis for that introductory scene.

Maybe you write the current scene with the character in a rose garden—because that perfectly typifies her ideal location—but for the purposes of your story you'll have to set it on a train. That's fine. Just adapt it. And maybe she's got a pressed rose in the book she's reading. ...

After you complete this scene you will know this character inside and out. You will be ready, actually, to bring him onstage. You may find yourself champing at the bit to get going. But you'll need to hold off a while. We still need to finish tracing out his inner journey.

THE INCITING INCIDENT

★ ★ ★

"HOW IT IS THAT I APPEAR BEFORE YOU IN A shape that you can see, I may not tell. I have sat invisible beside you many and many a day."

It was not an agreeable idea. Scrooge shivered, and wiped the perspiration from his brow.

"That is no light part of my penance," pursued the Ghost. "I am here to-night to warn you, that you have yet a chance and hope of escaping my fate. A chance and hope of my procuring, Ebenezer."

"You were always a good friend to me," said Scrooge. "Thank'ee!"

"You will be haunted," resumed the Ghost, "by Three Spirits."

Scrooge's countenance fell almost as low as the Ghost's had done.

"Is that the chance and hope you mentioned, Jacob?" he demanded, in a faltering voice.

"It is."

"I— I think I'd rather not," said Scrooge.

"Without their visits," said the Ghost, "you cannot
hope to shun the path I tread."
—**Charles Dickens** *A Christmas Carol*

With these dire words, Ebenezer Scrooge is sent on the detour of
his life. He is visited by three spirits who show him the error of
his ways. At the end of his odyssey, he is given the rare mercy of
being able to come back to his life and make a change. A chance
to live differently.

You're going to send your main character on just such a
detour. Somehow she has to get from her knot to her moment of
truth. But if left on her own, she will never take so much as the
first step toward that goal. You have to grab her by the scruff of
her neck and toss her headlong into the stream of the story.

The inciting event is the moment you, as story deity, board
the ship of this character's life, take over the helm, and steer him
right for the cataracts. It is the moment the main story intrudes
into the character's life in a way he cannot ignore.

What inciting events can you think of from fiction or film?
Scrooge is visited by the ghost of Jacob Marley. Dorothy's home
is carried away by a twister. Thirteen dwarves show up on Bilbo's
stoop and whisk him off toward adventure. Weatherman Phil
Connors finds himself reliving Groundhog Day over and over.
Lightning McQueen ends up in Radiator Springs and can't escape.
Novelist Paul Sheldon is abducted by his "number one fan" until he
agrees to write a book resurrecting that fan's favorite character. NFL
superstud Joe Kingman's ultimate bachelor life is interrupted by the
appearance of an eight-year-old daughter he never knew he had.

Zoom, off these characters go, careening in an unexpected
direction completely against their will. They don't have time
for this.

But you know they can't afford not to go on this journey.

BEFORE THE JOLT

Let's look at our full inner journey graphic again.

Your character is happily (or wretchedly) going about his business, somewhat hobbled by his knot but mostly settled with the status quo, when along comes something out of left field. He doesn't know it at the time, but this is the harbinger of hope for him, the sign that the universe cares for him and wants him to find health. At the moment it comes, the inciting event will seem to him to be a nuisance, an unwanted sidetrack that he can hopefully be done with quickly so he can get back to his (quietly dysfunctional) life.

But you won't let him.

As we'll discuss fully in part 2, I'm a big believer in what I call *establishing normal before disrupting normal.*

Beginning novelists often start their books with the main action of the story already front and center. Someone will come in and shoot everyone in the house, and the rest of the book will be about the lone survivor's journey from there. Or the heroine will announce she's leaving the hero and he'll spend the rest of the book trying to win her back.

That *in media res* (into the middle of affairs) strategy can sometimes work—sometimes extremely well—but it is more difficult to pull off. Most novelists would do well to stick with a linear, chronological approach, especially at first. If not done well, the *in media res* strategy fails because the reader simply doesn't care about the characters yet. Oh, too bad those strangers got shot. What a shame. Too bad that girl left what's-his-name. Bummer for him. In order for readers to feel the impact of the thing that happens to the main character and is supposed to propel the rest of the story, they have to care about him first. And you do that by spending some time in his life before the main plot intrudes on his world.

This holds true with the inner journey. You can't drop a little girl on the bachelor's doorstep until we've seen his life was like before the interruption. Otherwise we don't realize how different his life will become thanks to this new development. If the ghosts had shown up in poor Ebenezer's bedroom on page 1, we wouldn't have seen what a humbug he was—nor would there be any "before" with which to contrast his "after."

Begin thinking about your character's life. You've come up with a character Bible for her, so you know who she is and how she sees the world. You've produced a wonderful ultimate introduction for her, and that's fresh in your mind. You know her temperament and all the other layers of her personality. You even know what her initial condition is, how the story finds her when your tale begins. What you will have written in the first thirty or so pages of the book will simply show her in her natural habitat.

When she's adequately introduced so that the reader 1) knows who she is, 2) cares about her, and 3) has seen a bit of her knot, it's time to drop a bomb in her life.

PARDON THE INTERRUPTION

An inciting event can be anything, really. There's no right or wrong about it. There is one and only one qualification that will determine if something is a good inciting event: *It must divert the character toward his moment of truth.*

Tony would never have become a murderer and a fugitive if he'd not gone to the dance at the gym that night and met Maria. Frodo would never have come to the Cracks of Doom if the Ring hadn't come to him. Luke Skywalker would never have been there to launch the crucial proton torpedo if those droids hadn't rolled into his life. Moses would never have led the Children of Israel out of Egypt if he hadn't turned aside to see that mysteriously burning bush. The classic hard-boiled detective would never have gotten mixed up in the messes he gets mixed up in if the femme fatale hadn't shown up in his office.

As the marketing slogan for *Star Wars: Episode I* went, "Every saga has a beginning."

In every James Bond adventure, 007 gets his assignment. This launches him inexorably toward a major confrontation still far in the future. In every quest story, a herald arrives to bring a call to adventure, which sends the hero toward a certain showdown with the monster. Though there will be many plot twists and turns along the way, in a metaphorical, inner journey sense, there is a straight line between the inciting event and the moment of truth.

Think of the moment of truth as if it were a black hole. It is a mammoth void, a voracious throat sucking into it everything it can. Though your hero may not even be aware of the thing, the black hole's intense gravity snares him like a Jules Verne tentacle and begins to draw him near.

The inciting event is the thing that grabs hold of your hero like a tractor beam and drags her into the mouth of the beast.

Think about your main character's inner journey. You know where she is (initial condition) and where she will get to (moment of truth). Now consider what could happen that would divert her from her intended path and send her hurtling toward her destiny.

BACK UP A MINUTE

It might actually help to work backward. Consider starting with your character's moment of truth and then asking, "Well, what has to happen to get her to this moment? What will have to happen to get her right up to the brink of this decision?" Then back out from there. "What would have to happen to get her to the point where she's almost to the brink? And what would have to happen before that?" Keep backing up until you can see how to connect yourself up with her initial condition.

Let's walk backward through *Pygmalion* by George Bernard Shaw (or the Broadway musical, *My Fair Lady*, which is the same story).

Eliza Doolittle's moment of truth comes when Professor Higgins, who has trained her to speak not like the street urchin she initially was as but instead as the highborn lady he taught her to be, demands that she serve him as if she were his inferior: "Oh, by the way, Eliza, order a ham and a Stilton cheese, will you? And buy me a pair of reindeer gloves, number eights, and a tie to match that new suit of mine, at Eale & Binman's. You can choose the color."

He is saying, essentially, that she may have learned how to talk and act like a duchess, but she will always be a guttersnipe in his eyes. While another character (Colonel Pickering) has treated Eliza like a lady even when she was only a flower girl, Higgins saw her—sees her—as nothing more than an experiment or a pet. Pickering has given her self-respect.

Eliza says to Pickering:

> "You see, really and truly, apart from the things anyone can
> pick up (the dressing and the proper way of speaking, and
> so on), the difference between a lady and a flower girl is not
> how she behaves, but how she's treated. I shall always be a
> flower girl to Professor Higgins, because he always treats me
> as a flower girl, and always will; but I know I can be a lady to
> you, because you always treat me as a lady, and always will."

Her old way is to believe she is low and worthless. The new way
is to believe she has worth and power. This is her key decision—
which will she choose to go with? Higgins forces the decision by
looking at all she has accomplished and all she has become, and
attempting to put her down again.

Liza's response to his demands to buy the cheese and gloves
for him? "Buy them yourself."

Hurray, Eliza! You go, girl!

So we've seen how she resolves her big moment. Our task
now is to get from there to where she began, which is as a dirty
waif on the street, a low-caste denizen of the slums of London,
no better than a scullery maid. To do so, let's step backward
from the moment of truth.

You can do this even if you don't know the story. Use deduc-
tive reasoning, my dear Watson. If the moment of truth is a
decision between demanding self-respect as taught by Pickering and allowing herself to be treated as a trained monkey as
taught by Higgins, then I suppose both these men would have
to have trained her and had an immense influence in her life.
Excellent, so we will need to have a training time.

But how did that come to be? To find out, we have to step
backward from there. Somehow Eliza will have to have come
under the tutelage of these two men. There must've been some
arrangement. So we see that somehow she came to them or they

came to her to initiate this time of instruction. There's probably a scene or two in that.

But how did they come to know about each other? Gentlemen like this don't typically know women like Eliza. So there must've been some kind of encounter in which their worlds intersected. And in that encounter they must've brought up the idea of raising Eliza's behavior and speech so that she would pass for a lady. Wonder how that scene went.

See how we've done a little reverse engineering to figure out how to get from how she starts to where we want her to be in her moment of truth?

That scene in which Eliza meets Higgins and Pickering is the scene that sends all of them into a detour none of them had expected. It is the inciting event, the moment that diverts our main character into the primary action of the story and will lead directly to her moment of truth.

Work backward in your story. Backtrack from your main character's moment of truth until you reach the spot where he's stepped off the path he was walking down and pivoted over to this new trail. That moment when he diverts—or is diverted—is the inciting event.

Incidentally, there is a correlation between the inciting event in the hero's inner journey and the end of the first major segment of the plot. They're not the same (the inciting event usually comes much earlier in the story) but they are related. Both are like archways or gates leading us to the main action of the book.

WHAT MAKES A GOOD INCITING EVENT?

As I mentioned, the only real prerequisite for an inciting event is that it turns the hero onto a path that leads directly to her moment of truth. But there are some other qualities that enhance its effectiveness.

A good inciting event is unexpected. Most of the time, the inciting event is like the attack on Pearl Harbor. It is a surprise attack in which your character is ambushed and sent in an unexpected and (usually) unwanted direction. As we saw with Eliza, though, sometimes the diversion can come in the form of an opportunity, the chance of a lifetime, that the hero dare not pass up. Or, with Moses, the inciting event begins as a curiosity (why doesn't that bush burn up in the fire?). It's the same with the discovery of the portal in the wardrobe in *The Lion, the Witch, and the Wardrobe*. The point is that it's an exit off the expressway, a radical turn in a new direction.

A good inciting event has to do with the hero's knot, whether that's clear right away or not. The hero may witness a crime and get caught up in something awful, but she may not have a clue—until much later—that there's something she needs to learn about herself in it all. Phil Connors only wanted to leave Punxsutawney so he could get on with his career. He didn't realize he had entered the Twilight Zone and wouldn't be able to leave until he'd had an overhaul of his character. Good inciting events at first appear to be bothers out of the blue, but they end up being individually tailored for the hero.

A good inciting event represents a massive change for the hero, a huge wrench in the gears. It can't be a minor interruption that can be easily gotten rid of. When Joe Kingman's surprise daughter showed up on his doorstep, he tried to shut the door on her and go back to his life. But she was not to be gotten rid of so easily. Scrooge's ghosts could not be avoided. Jonah would've liked to take his chances in the ocean rather than be swallowed by a whale.

A good inciting event requires action from the hero. If the inciting event truly was the attack on Pearl Harbor, it would work only if that affected the hero. If the hero were a pygmy in Africa, Pearl Harbor wouldn't be the right inciting event. It has to be something that affects her directly and demands that she personally do something in response.

A good inciting event is one that works with everything else you want to do in the story. Said another way, be sure that whatever inciting event you choose is something you can bend the whole story around. If you want to write a fluffy chick-lit about girls who go shopping together, don't make the inciting event the main character's discovery that she has late-stage uterine cancer. Your inciting event has to match the rest of the story in tone and purpose.

FOR YOUR STORY

So, there your hero is, minding her business, walking along in her quiet dysfunction, making do with the best solution she's been able to find for her situation, when *wham,* along comes ... what? How do you want the gravitational tug of her moment of truth to reach out and grab her and begin pulling her in?

The inciting event is the harbinger of doom to your hero's old way of living. Like it or not, this interruption is the first cannonade in the war that has been brought to your hero's borders. But, just as much of our modern society would not be what it is had that sneak attack on Pearl Harbor never come, so your hero can never reach the defining, possibly saving moment of truth if he had been left alone. The inciting event is harbinger of doom—and herald of hope.

10

THE ESCALATION

★ ★ ★

Tybalt: Romeo, the hate I bear thee can afford / No better term than this,—thou art a villain.

Romeo: Tybalt, the reason that I have to love thee / Doth much excuse the appertaining rage / To such a greeting: villain am I none; / Therefore farewell; I see thou know'st me not.

Tybalt: Boy, this shall not excuse the injuries / That thou hast done me; therefore turn and draw.

Romeo: I do protest, I never injured thee, / But love thee better than thou canst devise, / Till thou shalt know the reason of my love: / And so, good Capulet,—which name I tender / As dearly as my own,—be satisfied.

Mercutio: O calm, dishonourable, vile submission! / Alla stoccata carries it away. *(Draws)* / Tybalt, you rat-catcher, will you walk?

Tybalt: What wouldst thou have with me?

Mercutio: Good king of cats, nothing but one of your nine / lives; that I mean to make bold

> withal, and as you / shall use me hereafter,
> drybeat the rest of the / eight. Will you
> pluck your sword out of his pitcher / by the
> ears? make haste, lest mine be about your /
> ears ere it be out.
> **Tybalt:** I am for you. *(Drawing)*
> —**William Shakespeare** *Romeo and Juliet*

There's nothing like a little escalation in fiction. It raises the stakes and fuels the fire. Here we see the mutual provocation that leads to Mercutio becoming a grave man.

In your main character's inner journey there must be escalation, as well. The end result of this intensification will bring her to a dire decision: her moment of truth.

There is, between the inciting incident and the moment of truth, a beautiful space. An ascent to glory. This upward climb is the heart of your main character's inner journey—which makes it the heart of your novel. In plot terms, which we'll discuss in part 2, most of the hero's escalation takes place in Act II, the chewy middle of your book.

Here's our graphic:

At a glance you can see how important, how central, the escalation phase is. If the inciting event gets the character arc going and the moment of truth is its culmination, then what's left is the real meat of the story. Here, the old way and the new way duke it out. I often refer to it as an escalating arms race.

MUTUALLY ASSURED DECONSTRUCTION

In keeping with our *Romeo and Juliet* theme, here's a bit from *West Side Story*:

Riff: We challenge you to a rumble. All out, once and for all. Accept?

Bernardo: On what terms?

Riff: Whatever terms you're callin', buddy boy. You crossed the line once too often.

Bernardo: You started it.

Riff: Who jumped A-rab this afternoon?

Bernardo: Who jumped me the first day I moved here?

Riff: Who asked you to move here?

Bernardo: Who asked you?

Snowboy: Move where you're wanted!

A-Rab: Back where ya came from!

Action: Spics!

Pepe: Micks!

Indio: Wop!

Bernardo: We accept!

Riff: Time:

Bernardo: Tomorrow?

Riff: The river.

Bernardo: Under the highway.

[They shake.]

Riff: Weapons!

Bernardo: Weapons…

Riff: You call.

Bernardo: Your challenge.

Riff: Afraid to call?

Bernardo: …Sticks.

Riff: …Rocks.

Bernardo: …Poles.

Riff: …Cans.

Bernardo: …Bricks.

> **Riff:** ...Bats.
> **Bernardo:** ...Clubs.
> **Tony:** Bottles, knives, guns! *[They stare.]* What a
> coop full of chickens!
> —**Ernest Lehman** *West Side Story (screenplay)*

These guys are so angry at each other that sticks aren't good enough for their fight. So one suggests rocks. The other ramps it up by suggesting poles. The first guy trumps poles with cans. And up it goes from there.

This is how the escalation phase will go in your main character's inner journey.

Remember, your hero has a problem. This knot is poisoning her, even if she doesn't know it. She has settled into an injurious pattern of life that, if unchecked, will eventually spell doom (in one sense or another). Go back and read your notes for this character's knot. What is it? How is it harming her?

If you've chosen a good knot, it will be something that can't be remedied easily. His knot can't be something like the fact that his ski boots are unbuckled and if he doesn't fix them he might lose a ski. It has to be something deeply ingrained in his psyche: a fear, an anger (which is really just fear, anyway), or a cognitive dissonance that will eventually tear him in two.

A good knot, in other words, is not easily untied. To use our medical metaphor, it's a tumor that has wrapped itself around an organ or major artery. To go military, which is the best language for this chapter, it is an enemy deeply entrenched in an underground bunker.

To dislodge this enemy, we can't simply shoot at it. We can't even just drop normal bombs on it and hope to prevail. We can try, but we'll find that the enemy is too well dug in for that to work. We'll have to bring in larger and larger bombs, including the mother of all bunker busters, to take out this enemy.

This is how it will go for your main character in the escalation phase. She's entrenched in her old way. It may not be great, but it beats every alternative she's tried. Then into her relative peace comes an unexpected attack (the inciting event). It's a nuisance, most likely, but nothing that can't be ignored. Probably. Hopefully. But the nuisance doesn't go away. Her first attempts to get past it are thwarted. So she ratchets it up to the next level. Now it's a major annoyance.

In *The Sisterhood of the Traveling Pants*, Tibby just wants to be left alone to make her movie. She's angry and depressed and wants to shoot her "suckumentary" about how bad her life is. Then this girl Bailey comes over and starts asking lots of questions about the movie, wanting to be her assistant. Tibby tries to make her leave, but Bailey is persistent. She won't let it go. Bailey becomes Tibby's problem, this irritating nuisance who can't take a hint.

That's what you've got to do to your character. You've got to follow the inciting event with an onslaught from this new thing in his life. It's like an invasion. The inciting event was the invasion that gave the enemy a beachhead, and now he's pouring troops into the breach. Suddenly it's a major problem.

The Puerto Ricans keep arriving in Jets' territory (*West Side Story*). More and more boys slip away from Ralph's group to join Jack's (*Lord of the Flies*). No matter what he does, Gregor can't convince his family that he is not a large insect (*The Metamorphosis*). Though Frodo may wish to avoid leaving the Shire, evil spreads—servants of the Dark Lord encroach ever closer, endangering his friends and family (*The Lord of the Rings*).

It quickly becomes apparent that more radical measures are called for.

THE DUEL

Let's go all figurative for a moment. Your character has a knot that has caused him to live in a less than ideal way. The entire purpose of the story is to cause him to see that this old way is hurting him and that there is a new way he might try, and to make him choose. The inciting event is the first fusillade in the war that has been thrust upon him. Everything else between those first shots and the final showdown at the moment of truth is a duel between the old and new ways.

This duel is chiefly characterized by escalation. Hero wants to stay as he is. New way comes in and tries to knock him out of the old way. Hero fights back, digs in deeper to the old way, goes more extreme. That seems to solve the problem for the moment. But the new way strikes back, this time in a way that gets around his previous solution, so that won't work anymore. Hero escalates, playing a card he hasn't wanted to play. That gains him some relief, but it's clear this challenger isn't done either.

Sure enough, the new way comes back with an even stronger attack. Now he's got to pull out all the stops to defeat it. He's being pushed further and further into his dysfunction—all because he needs to protect himself from what he fears. The duel continues to escalate until our hero is broken. Either he's exhausted his last resort and it has failed or he's crossed a line that has shocked him. Finally, he understands what the new way is offering and how the old way is hurting him.

That's his moment of truth, his opportunity to change. Before that, he was just trying to hold onto his previous solution. Along the way, he might've seen some things in the new way that were appealing, nevertheless he hasn't let himself seriously consider it. But now he can. Now he must. And that is where you've been trying to get him from page 1.

None of it would've happened without the escalating arms race. If the inciting event had not been followed by an influx of enemy pressure, he could've gone back to his old way and tried to forget about that little interruption. *The escalating duel is the vehicle that drives him from his dysfunction to his opportunity to change.*

I GOT YOU, BABE

A great example of the escalating arms race is in the movie *Groundhog Day*. Phil Connors is an arrogant, self-absorbed narcissist who claims he's soon going to leave his job as a meteorologist at a Pittsburgh TV station to make it to the big time. For the last time (he hopes) he is forced to go to Punxsutawney to cover the Groundhog Day celebration—because Punxsutawney Phil (the groundhog) is the world's most famous weatherman. So he gets in the van with a cameraman and a new producer, Rita, to whom Phil is attracted, and they head off to see the groundhog.

After filming the ceremony and retiring for the night, Phil wakes up the next morning ready to go home. Except he discovers that it's Groundhog Day. Again. This is the inciting event. But Phil tries to brush it off. He marks it up to bizarre sense of déjà vu and forges through the day again. The next morning he wakes up and it is, you guessed it, Groundhog Day again. No one else realizes the day is being repeated. Only Phil knows what's happening.

So begins a beautiful deconstruction of Phil Connors' character. A character that had been sorely in need of deconstruction. Watch the duel escalate in this rendering of the story:

At first, Phil tries to escape his situation. Day after identical day he hopes to wake from his dream. First he's downcast, seeking solace in alcohol. He then decides to take advantage of his plight by gorging himself on sweets, joyriding, robbing an armored car, seducing women, and essentially living it up. He soon gets bored and realizes he is unfulfilled. He becomes depressed, going so far as to initiate an elaborate series of suicides. Despite it all, he always wakes up and it's the same day, again and again.

See how it's an escalating duel? Phil believes himself to be an unstoppable force, but this supernatural predicament he's encountered is proving to be an immovable object.

His attempts to escape the recurring day become more and more desperate until he eventually comes to suspect that he must find love to break the spell and sets out upon the final leg of his internal journey.

Groundhog Day is the clearest illustration I've seen of the escalation phase of the inner journey. Plus, it's just a great movie. Watch it whenever you want to see what an escalation duel looks like.

ESCALATION VACILLATION

It's one thing to hear about the escalation in the figurative terms I've used in this chapter or to see it illustrated in an example, but it's something else to know how to do it in your own book.

They key is to have a firm grip on two things: what your hero's old way will eventually do to her if left unchecked and what bright future the new way is trying to get her to receive.

The whole point of the escalation phase is to show your hero the error of her ways. She wants to keep living in her dysfunction, but you will not allow it. You strike her with a redemptive fist until she is forced to admit that her old way is hurting her and will lead nowhere good. You are ushering her to the moment when she will decide once and for all whether to turn her back on the old way or submerge back into it, forever lost. Whatever you choose for the new way must be something that

135

perfectly points out the failure of her old way and offers her a better future.

A classic tragic flaw in literature is ambition. This was Macbeth's problem. Let's say your heroine's knot is ambition, as well. For reasons known to you, she pursues advancement in her career above everything else. She is known as a backstabber, brown noser, and snitch—anything to get ahead.

Your job as story god is to challenge her ambition. You want her to see that she is alienating herself from family and friends and she will end up possibly rich and at the top of the ladder, but alone and afraid of all the enemies she's made to get there. You engineer the events of the story so she can see that there is an alternative: a life in which she is less successful in her career but much happier in general, a life filled with loved ones and good moments she'd otherwise have to sacrifice.

Those are the two contenders in this heavyweight bout. The champion is her old way—success at any cost. The challenger is the new way—slowing down to enjoy the "riches" of good relationships and a contented life.

There has to be a reason she's settled on this old way. It helps her overcome a fear about herself or right an old injustice or prove her mother wrong or make her father proud. It has to be deeply personal and ingrained, but toxic, like poison slowly inching its way to her heart.

Now, how are you going to get her to believe that this new way of peace and simple enjoyment is going to be better for her than her old way? The old way may have its disadvantages, but it has the primary advantage of helping her do the main thing she wants done: proving her mother wrong (or whatever it might be).

You know what her moment of truth is going to look like and you've already determined her inciting event. The task now is to lift the fight to new heights. She's going to try to immediately discount the inciting event and get back to climbing the ladder of success. So what are you going to use to block her from doing that? How are you going to escalate?

Maybe your inciting event is something like this: While driving to work one morning she is checking her stocks on her iPhone and ends up rear-ending a minivan. She gets out and finds that it's a young mother—about the hero's own age—with three small children in the back, all crying. She helps get the children and mother out of the car. One of the children, a little girl, gives her something in thanks—a dress-up tiara, maybe. Our hero gets everything patched up and leaves for her job.

She's the aggressive lioness-woman when she walks into the office. She sits at her desk and drops her things—only to see the tiara tumble to the rug. On a whim, she calls her insurance agent to be sure things will be taken care of for that family. She learns the address of the family and finds out they were uninsured. It tugs at her heart a little because what if the children had been hurt? Who would take care of them? No time for that, though. Got a meeting to lead, a committee to chair, a power lunch with the new VP, and, at 2:00, she's firing three people. Off she goes.

Until something makes her think of the little girl again.

See how this could go? I think Jodie Foster should play this woman, actually. A tough broad whose tender heart has been hidden away for protection, but something is coaxing it out.

The escalation is the interplay between a comfortable, if vaguely dissatisfying, lifestyle on the one hand, and an alternative that feels different and incorrect, but winsome somehow, on the other. This interplay intensifies as the story progresses. Indeed, it *is* the story. Old way fights to maintain control. New way keeps finding ways around the defenses. She bounces back and forth between them ... until it all comes to a head.

Scout vacillates between courage and cowardice in the racial tensions of *To Kill a Mockingbird*. In *Titanic*, Rose vacillates between the old way (marrying a rich man to save her family's status) and the new way (running off with a poor but roguish artist). Edna, in *The Awakening*, vacillates between adherence to the emotional repression society demands of her and the liberation she's discovered in the story. Novelist Alex Rover vacillates between agoraphobe and adventurer when a little girl across the world calls to her for help (*Nim's Island*).

You see the key element here, right? Vacillation. That doesn't mean the character is weak minded. It just means that where there was once only one power in the character's quadrant of the universe, now there are two. Everything isn't as settled as the hero once thought. Things are up in the air, in play.

What are the two opponents in your character's inner journey? How will they fight one another? How will the new way show itself strong enough that it causes your hero to begin vacillating between the two?

WHEN DO CHARACTERS CHANGE?

Nobody likes change. We get set in our ways. We like the comfortable and the familiar.

Yet we're barraged by pleas to change. Don't be happy with your old car; buy this new one. Don't eat at home; eat out. Don't eat at *that* restaurant; eat at this one. Don't vote for that guy; vote for this one. Don't watch that show; watch this one. Call now! Don't wait! Offer ends soon. Operators are standing by. Supplies are limited.

There are so many appeals to change weighing upon us that we develop a certain resistance—even beyond the one we would normally have. If we didn't, we'd be tossed about by every strong personality that came along. We'd be spineless, directionless, and quickly relieved of our paychecks. (Wait, that *is* what's happening!)

Your characters are just like you and me. They don't like to change. They may be aware that things are not ideal in their lives, but they haven't found a better solution than the one they're going with now, so they're going to stick with it, thank you very much.

Humans—real or fictional—do not easily change. They actively resist change. In fact, the more you push them to change, the more they dig in and resist.

In order to bring about change, a character has to be convinced that his current way of doing things is not good. That's what the escalation phase is all about: convincing your main character that he needs to change. Indeed, that he can't afford not to change.

People resist change until the cost of staying the same becomes too great. Characters will not change until it hurts too much not to.

Picture a woman who runs a music store. We'll call her Kate. The store is in a good location in a good part of town. Kate's parents founded the store thirty years ago and she's always known she would take over the store, which she did seven years ago. Things have gone mostly well since then. The doors are still open, after all. But sales are in a downward trend. If Kate were honest, she'd have to admit that they've been trending that way for pretty much the whole time she's been at the helm of the store.

She's concerned. It's led her to try all manner of sales and promotions and album signings with local musicians, but nothing has done more than add a blip to sales. She knows her core constituency, so she works to reach a bigger number of those people. She's adjusted the store to carry more of the CDs and related products that appeal to that audience. She's made the store like it's always been, but more so. More focused. But nothing helps.

She's had offers to buy the store. Kate always sent those people packing, of course. I mean, the very idea! What would her parents think if she sold out? Music stores all around her are closing. The big box stores are taking over. And there's this "new" thing called the Internet. Online stores and MP3s are being sold online for prices that would break her. Maybe she should've sold the store when she had the chance.

If things don't turn around quick, she's not going to have money to pay her employees, much less run ads or even buy new inventory for the shelves. The store is dying on the vine and nothing she does seems to make a difference.

Then comes a particularly low day, a day when only her tears on the phone with the utilities person caused them to turn the power back on. The few people that do drive into the parking lot see the lights off and think the store is closed, so they drive on. Now Kate's got her employees standing out in the cold waving down passersby and holding, "Yes, we're open!" signs. She can't bear to bring them in and tell them she's going to have to fire them all. Her parents are rolling over in their graves, she's sure of it.

Up steps a man who says he would like to talk to her about possibly buying the store.

Suddenly, it's not such a terrible idea. Suddenly, Kate's interested: "Step right into my office." It turns out that he wants to keep it open as a music store. He's got an idea to change it into a music store-bookstore-café thing using print-on-demand machines to print up books people order from online catalogues right there in the store. The books are printed and bound as customers browse MP3s and sip lattes while sitting in giant overstuffed chairs by a fire. Local musicians will regularly play in the store. He agrees to keep her entire staff on payroll. There might even be an assistant manager's position for her.

"Where do I sign?"

A change she wouldn't even contemplate before is now something she can't wait to do. Why? Because it has become too painful not to change.

That's what you've got to do to your character. He wants to stay the same. You must bring the pain. Rain the pain. Flood the pain. Raise the stakes and escalate the struggle until now it hurts worse to resist the change than to consider it.

Keep in mind that you're not forcing her to change. Kate could've gone pigheaded and refused to take this offer, though it would cause her to lose in every way that's important to her. Still, she could've. Part of her actually wants to play it that way. The memory of her parents would at least be honored that she'd gone down with the ship. Right? But would they really want that?

That point where she's actually questioning it, where she's finally contemplating what the new way might look like, is the place you're trying to get your character to. That's her moment of truth. That's her chance at redemption.

But she never would've gotten there if you hadn't acted like a torturer and thrown her on the rack, cranking up the tension one peg at a time. Bring the pain.

LITTLE MOMENTS OF TRUTH ALL ALONG THE WAY

In a sense, your main character will have multiple moments of truth during the course of the story—at the inciting event, for instance. The first time the new way intrudes on the character and suggests he could be different, he has the option of choosing the new path.

As soon as the ghost of Jacob Marley appeared to Ebenezer Scrooge, Scrooge could've said, "Okay, I give. I'll be generous and kind now!" As soon as Lightning McQueen found himself in Radiator Springs, he could've said, "Okay, you win—I'll be considerate of others!" The first moment Einar's granddaughter walked onstage (in *An Unfinished Life*), he could've foresworn all his bitterness to embrace the family he thought he'd lost.

But that wouldn't be believable. (Plus, the story would be over on page 27.) Your character has to be so deeply entrenched in the old way that it will take a lot more than a gentle knocking on the door to get him to change. It's going to take the equivalent of a wrecking ball.

Every time the old way meets up with a counterattack from the new way, the character faces a minor moment of truth. He may not be ready to change. The pain of staying the same may not be great enough to make him truly contemplate a change. But the fact remains that each new blow from the challenger gives the hero an opportunity to go that way.

As soon as Phil Connors recognizes he's stuck in a recurring Groundhog Day, he has the chance to realize he is all about the wrong things. But he's too far gone for that. He can't even hear that. If someone told him exactly what he needed to do to change, he wouldn't have been able to seriously contemplate it.

For years I had been told about a certain nonfiction book. It's one of those books everyone wants to have read but no one wants to read. I'd heard of it and figured it would probably help me, but I had other pressing priorities. Years later, I went through something pivotal in my life and someone recommended the book to me again. This time I was ready to hear it. I ran out and bought the book and read it like a drowning man trying to stay afloat. It changed my life.

I've since tried to recommend it to others. But they all have other pressing priorities. I've realized that you can't accept the message of this book until you're ready for it. And you can't make someone be ready for it. If I'd read that book years ago, I don't believe it would've had the same impact on me. I wasn't ready for it.

So it is with your main character. She needs to hear the thing the new way has to offer. But she doesn't believe she does. It's your job as author to make her ready. You have to take her through successive waves of beat downs in which she tries harder and harder to resist the new way and stick with the old way. You have to show her in an ever-escalating situations that her old way simply will not work this time. Everything she tries ends up failing or backfiring. She gets more and more desperate. You must, in a sense, break her. You must bring her to the point where she's finally willing and able to listen to an alternative.

You do that by giving her multiple little moments of choice, all leading to the big one at the end. You're essentially saying, each time, *now* are you willing to listen to me? She says no— every time but once.

SYMBOLS OF CHANGE

We're not thinking about plot yet, but you can already begin playing with ideas for things you might do in the external plot to *personify* the old and new ways set before your main character.

So, for instance, if your main character is struggling with a selfishness that is making him ever more isolated, you could have him encounter a homeless man dying alone and unmourned in the street. This is a picture of what he might become. You could come up with several symbols of his possible future: a successful corporate executive who kills himself out of loneliness, an old woman languishing without family or visitors in a nursing home, a dog so mean no one wants it.

Perhaps our hero feels some indefinable connection to the dog and so brings it home. Despite his best efforts he can't domesticate it, so he's left with no option but to take it back to the pound, though he knows they will put it down.

In most cases, you don't want to be too overt about this. No *that could be me* thoughts in his mind (or worse: "That could be *you,* dummy" comments from others). Just let these symbols be there as subtle thematic echoes that some readers will catch but most will not.

Think of ways to portray the new way too. Using our selfish lonely guy example, he might encounter a little girl who gets a dollar and immediately goes around handing out pennies to the other kids in the park. Maybe he meets his exact opposite: a penniless but beloved man, who is perhaps dying but surrounded by loved ones and at peace with his life. Maybe his life is invaded by a flower child who is all about "paying it forward." The point is to find ways to illustrate his possible positive future.

Some of the examples you choose could actually reinforce his desire to not change. For instance, maybe he idealizes someone he thinks is working the old way famously. In *Ghosts of Girlfriends Past,* the lead character reveres his Uncle Wayne, who was a confirmed womanizer. But Uncle Wayne appears to him as a ghost and tells him he wasn't as happy as he always let on.

Or perhaps you could present an unattractive example of the new way, like a judgmental zealot for a religion the hero is being led to consider converting to. He would point to that person and say, "Why would I want that? No, thanks. I think I'll stay with my old life."

Think of ways you might externalize the hero's inner struggle. Personify the new way and the old way with one or more characters—human or otherwise—in the story. You don't have to think of who exactly they might be, since we haven't yet talked about what genre or era you might be writing in. But you can brainstorm about how you might put skin on these ideas.

BACK IT UP

In the previous chapter we found our inciting event by walking backward from the moment of truth. The same exercise will help us here. Actually, if you did that in the last chapter, you've already walked right through your escalation phase for this character.

Recall what you discovered as you backtracked through your story to find your inciting event. What were the "Well, I guess this and this would have to happen" bits between your moment of truth and the inciting event? Those can form the outline of your escalation phase.

Sommersby is the story of Laurel, a woman whose husband is reported to have died in the Civil War. Yet he returns, much changed by war. So changed, in fact, that even Laurel is not sure this is the same man. They look the same and talk the same, but her husband had been abusive and this man is not.

So let's start at Laurel's moment of truth and walk backward through the story to trace the escalation. The moment of truth is when this man is going to be hung for a murder her husband committed years ago. The man—who may or may not be her true husband—longs to see Laurel in the crowd watching the lynching. He says he can go through with it if she's there. She must decide whether or not to go out for him, because doing so will mean she has given her heart fully to him, something she could never do to the man she married.

Jumping all the way back to the beginning, the inciting event in this story is when this man, ostensibly her husband, strode back into Laurel's life.

So what happened in between those two points? Without knowing the rest of the story, we can determine the broad strokes of the middle section, the escalating arms race, by walking backward through it.

If the moment of truth is Laurel vacillating between her budding love for this person, whoever he is, on the one hand, and her old hate for her true husband and the suspicion that this is an imposter, on the other, then we can assume some things. We can assume that this person has shown himself to be different from her husband. We can assume that he has been kind where the other had been cruel. We can assume that Laurel has spent most of the story in anger and suspicion, but has slowly begun to risk loving again.

See how scenes already begin suggesting themselves?

If he's being hung for a crime committed before the war, we can assume the law has caught up to him after not catching up to him for most of the story. We can assume he's been convincing enough playing the role of her husband that whatever legal system they live under has determined he is the man accused of the crime.

Though we don't know if this man is really her husband or not, we can imagine what must be going through his mind if he is not her husband. If he tells the truth and admits he is not her husband, Laurel will have been living in sin with someone she's not married to (and everyone will know it) and he will be exposed as an imposter. If he stays silent, he will be executed for a crime he didn't commit.

Stepping backward from there, we know that this man has to have been living with Laurel for some time, getting to know her and showing that he's not the same, perhaps expressing love for her. We can assume that at the beginning she treated him as she would have treated her husband, using whatever defenses or dysfunctions had been in place before he left. We can assume she's been trying to figure out if he's really her husband, and has perhaps been testing him with his knowledge of their lives together before the war.

We can envision that first day and night after his return, when Laurel is trying to decide if this person is really her husband and should be allowed to stay in the house.

And *that* brings us all the way to the inciting event, when he steps back into her life.

ESCALATOR

The fun of *Sommersby* is its middle, that beautiful space between inciting event and moment of truth.

So it is with your book. Your main character's inner journey has an escalation phase at its heart. This is the fun of your story, the lab counter where you do your experimentation and creation. It is the boxing ring where you watch two Rock 'Em Sock 'Em Robots go at it. It is the field of battle between two powerful armies. Everything that comes before is setup and everything that comes after is climax and resolution. But the heart of your story is the escalating arms race between the old way, whose end is death (or dysfunction), and the new way, whose end is life.

Watching your character try to bring this crisis to a quick conclusion—and watching the new way not let him—is the primary treasure you give the readers of your novel.

11

THE FINAL STATE

★ ★ ★

STUDYING PUG, MARTIN SAID, "YOU SPEAK calmly enough of this. Doesn't my claim to the throne disturb you at all?"

Pug shook his head. "You would have no way of knowing, but I was counted among the most powerful men in Tsuranuanni. My word was in some ways more important than any king's command. I think I know what power can do, and what sort of men seek it. I doubt you have much personal ambition as such, unless you've changed a great deal since I lived in Crydee. If you take the crown, it will be for what you believe are good reasons. It may be the only way to prevent civil war, for should you choose the mantle of King, Lyam will be the first to swear fealty. Whatever the reason, you would do your best to act wisely. And if you take the purple, you will do your best to be a good ruler."

Martin looked impressed. "You have changed much, Squire Pug, more than I would have expected."

—Raymond E. Feist, *Magician*

We come at last to the end of your hero's inner journey. She was happy in her dysfunction, but you came along and blasted her out of it. You forced her to see how the old way was slowly poisoning her, and you showed her an alternative that would require a change on her part—and quite possibly a risk—but that would be so much healthier for her. You brought her to the threshold and you forced her to choose. But it was her free choice.

The last bit of her journey to write is the final state. It is simply a depiction of what she is like after making her choice.

THE NEW ME

In the story excerpted above, Pug was a young man who had just discovered his magical abilities when he was taken against his will to an alternate world. He served as a slave until he was able to learn that world's magic system. Then he rose in power and status. The two worlds engaged in war and Pug was able to return to his home, but only after incredible changes had been wrought in his character. He left as no more than an unwanted orphan and he returned as lord and master, having been matured by suffering, loss, and achievement.

Your main character will undergo a similar journey. He will not be the same person he was at the beginning of the book. *The journey itself defines character.* Indeed, that's the point of the whole story.

When the final curtain is about to fall, it is time to redepict this character. Just as you wrote a soliloquy scene describing who he was at the outset of the story, so you should write one for him at the end. A comparison of the two scenes will clearly reveal how he has changed.

What you write in this scene—whether it's an idealized gazetteer like we did before or a contextualized event you can actually include in your book—will be determined by what he has chosen in his moment of truth.

If he chose "wrong" in his moment of truth (i.e., if he chose to side finally with the old way) his final state scene will show the negative results of his choice. Perhaps he'll die like Kurtz in *Heart of Darkness,* uttering "The horror. The horror." If he chose "right" (if he sided with the new way), perhaps he'll die like Theoden in *The Return of the King,* saying, "My body is broken. I go to my fathers. And even in their mighty company I shall not now be ashamed. I felled the black serpent. A grim morn, and a glad day, and a golden sunset!"

Not that your hero has to die! I'm just saying ...

As we'll see in part 2, the last scene of your book is where you'll tie everything off. The reader finds out who lived, who is recovering from injuries, who got what medals, who hooked up with whom, and the rest. We'll also see the "after" stage of one or more main characters.

If your main character is a town in Oklahoma, metaphorically speaking, and the story is the tornado that rips through it, the final state is the aftermath, those brutal aerial photos of the town the morning after the storm.

Whatever she chose in her moment of truth, her final state has a direct correlation to her initial condition. She's either the opposite of what she was then or she's what she was then times ten.

If at the beginning she had been dealing with a fear of being rejected, at the end she will either be happy with herself and able to take risks in relationships or she will be so utterly consumed with a fear of rejection that she will take measures to never be rejected again, perhaps even by becoming a prostitute (who doesn't always charge).

If at the beginning, your hero has been struggling with anger, at the end he will either be able to let things go and just enjoy the moment or he will be so overwhelmed with anger that he will do something radical, like going on a shooting spree.

The final state is both a reflection and an amplification of the initial condition. Both potential futures were alive in the hero at the beginning of the story. How he ends up will be either exactly like he was at the beginning, only ten times worse, or it will be its polar opposite.

Perhaps the most famous character arc in modern pop culture is that of Anakin Skywalker (Darth Vader). He had both good and evil in him but the latter had almost driven out the former. His son appealed to the good and, at Vader's moment of truth, Vader turned to the good side. Though it cost him his life, he found redemption.

Another well-known character arc is that of Gollum (Sméagol) in *The Lord of the Rings*. Again, he had both good and evil in him and the latter had all but driven out the former, and again someone appealed to the good. But Gollum ultimately chose evil and was destroyed.

What will it be for your character? The whole story is designed to get her to that moment of truth when she can decide to go with the redemptive choice or the destructive choice. The rest is aftermath. Has she chosen the glorious peace and joy that comes from accepting the right way or the flaming plunge into darkness that comes from choosing the wrong way?

Your reader hopes your character will choose the right way, but whatever she chooses, you reader will be captivated by the final state. There's something fascinating about watching people make choices and live with the fallout.

Perhaps that is why we read fiction.

WHAT GOES INTO A GOOD FINAL STATE SCENE?

The purpose of a final state scene is to show what has become of the hero as a result of the choice he made in his moment of truth.

Even before you know what your plot or even your genre will be, you can decide how to depict your character after the storm. Later, you can change the costumes or setting to go with the external action of the book, but right now we're finishing off his inner journey.

The essential element of a final state scene is to reveal the character's emotional well-being in light of the decision he made at the moment of truth. Is he happy now, or more miserable?

There might be a touch of madness or abandon to her reaction, since she is essentially emerging from—or plunging more deeply into—a mind-rending psychotic episode. Like maybe she runs around laughing all the time in her new joy and freedom, as Mr. Banks did at the end of *Mary Poppins* or Scrooge did at the end of *A Christmas Carol*. Or she might laugh maniacally as she pours oil on her head and lights the fire, as Denethor did near the climax of *The Return of the King*.

The point, you see, is that the moment of truth is over. That all-consuming instant of cognitive dissonance has finally been resolved. One side or the other has won out—has pushed him off the fence once and for all—and that side will reign supreme at the end of the story in this character's life.

Look for an extreme way of expressing this as you contemplate the final state scene. You might tone it down when you actually write it for the book, but knowing what it would be in excess will help you write it in moderation. If he feels *free* here at the end, for instance, find a way to express that freedom: jumping out of an airplane, singing from a housetop, running naked through the forest. If he feels more trapped than ever, find an ultimate way to express that: closing himself into a closet, wedging himself into a tight place, tearing up his passport.

The idea is to externalize what he's feeling on the inside. How will your main character be after he makes his big choice?

We'll talk about this more in part 2, but you will often combine your final state scene with your falling action scene. The falling action (dénouement) scene is how the external plot story is tied off. The final state scene is how the internal inner journey story is tied off. You will usually do them together.

If you need to show how the war turned out and how the character feels at the end, you can have her presiding over the enemy's ratification of the surrender treaty while simultaneously being on cloud nine because of what she decided in her moment of truth. If you need to show that three of the four couples successfully reconciled but the fourth didn't, and that your main character (part of the sad fourth) is now deeper into depression than ever, you can show a joint reaffirmation of marriage vows scene during which your hero leaves the ceremony to cry in private.

Look back at your character's *initial condition* and then do the math. Either give us that times negative one, to show how far in the opposite direction she's come, or give us that times ten to show how much worse she is now than at the beginning.

A CIRCULAR ARGUMENT

I'm a big believer in circularity in fiction. Circularity is when you take a moment at the end to refer back to the beginning. You can use it at the beginning and ending of a scene, section, or entire novel.

This is more than just showing that your character was lonely at the beginning but has friends at the end. Circularity in this sense is re-creating some moment from the beginning and then showing how she deals with it differently at the end. Set it up in the same way and bring her to the same moment, but then show her making a different choice.

In chapter 8 (Initial Condition) we talked about a woman who was so afraid of abandonment she made all her potential friends and boyfriends sign legally binding documents promising to never leave or forsake her, on penalty of the forfeiture of a portion of their assets. So maybe her introductory scene shows her doing just that. A young man arrives at her apartment to take her out for dinner. She invites him in and sits him down at a table with a pen and paper before him. "Sign it," she says. We find out it's the contract promising not to forsake her.

Fast-forward to the very end of the story, after she's been through everything and made her crucial choice, and write a concluding scene in which you re-create that first scene. A man arrives to take her out to dinner. She invites him in and sits him down at a table with a pen and paper. "Sign it," she says. Only now we see that it's simply a birthday card for a mutual friend. He's signed his name next to hers in a free expression of affection. It's very similar to the first scene, but now she's very different.

Or perhaps, if she chose differently in her moment of truth, she sits him down to sign something, but when he reaches for the pen she handcuffs him to the table and laughs with insane glee.

Fun with fiction.

Ebenezer Scrooge was all humbug in the face of Bob Cratchit's son, Tiny Tim, but at the end he treats the boy with kindness and becomes a second father to him. In *Groundhog Day*, Phil Connors steps in the same ice water-filled pothole every day. But when he makes an internal change, he remembers to step extra wide to avoid that pothole the next time.

Chapter 1 of my third novel, *Fatal Defect*, begins at two in the morning with the hero up with his little daughter, who has fallen asleep on his shoulder after reading picture books. His paternal moment is interrupted by a crisis that he must deal with in his underground communications center. Then the whole of the novel intervenes. The last chapter of the book returns him to his home. It is again two in the morning and he is up reading picture books with his little girl. But this time he does not get up for anything.

Now, every novel you write doesn't have to have bookend scenes like this. You can serve circularity well simply by hearkening back to something early in the book. My fourth novel, *Operation: Firebrand*, begins with this line: "Today I am going to kill a man in cold blood." The book ends not with that scene re-created but with him thinking back to that day and realizing that his ending state is a whole lot better than that day he got up to kill a man in cold blood.

Circularity makes your book feel complete, holistic, planned. It makes it look like you had the whole thing perfectly formed in your head before you penned a single word. It feels gift-wrapped, tied off, and intentional. You'll look like a genius.

So here at the end of your character's arc, read over your initial condition scene and see if there is some way you can echo that earlier moment to show how far the character has come.

JOURNEY'S END

And that, my dear friend, is the end of your main character's inner journey.

| Initial Condition | Knot | Inciting Event | | Moment of Truth | Final State |

To recap (and to apply a little circularity myself), the essential dyad of a character's inner journey is between the knot and the moment of truth. Your main character is afflicted with a hurtful "sin" that would, if uncorrected, eventually lead him to some form of destruction. The whole purpose of the story is to make him aware of this problem and show him a better way. It's all about getting him to his moment of truth, because that is where he can finally make a freewill decision between the old way and the new way.

Everything else exists to serve this moment. The initial condition is how his knot is affecting him before the moment of truth. The inciting event is the thing that detours him toward his moment of truth. The escalation is the swelling battle between the old way and the new way, leading him to the moment of truth. And the final state is what the character is like because of what he decided in the moment of truth.

Your book is about your main character's moment of truth, those two hundred words in which she makes her choice. All the other 99,800 words in your book are there just to set up that moment.

When you have created your main character's inner journey, you have determined 75 percent of your book. Your novel is *about* this inner journey and the inner journey is about the moment of truth. Just as the other elements of the inner journey exist to serve the moment of truth, so the other 25 percent of your book exists to serve the inner journey. Through plot, genre, backdrop, subplots, and more, all we're doing is decorating the inner journey. Supporting it. Amplifying it.

If you're a plot-first novelist, like me, I hope you're feeling encouraged right now. You've crafted a marvelously detailed central character for your book, and much of the process has felt like—and actually is—plot building. A character arc *is* a plot.

If you're a character firster, I hope this process has shown you aspects of your character that you otherwise might not have thought of. I hope you're seeing too that something you're comfortable doing has already gotten you 75 percent into something you might not be as comfortable doing. Your character building has created a plot structure.

Now let's have some fun deciding how best to present this masterpiece of character transformation. If the inner journey is the diamond, let's craft the perfect setting to show it off.

Part 2

MARVELOUS PLOTS

P*lot Versus Character* begins with the theory that some writers are born with character ideas floating through their heads and other writers are more likely to have plot ideas. Whichever kind of writer you are, you're reading this book probably because you realize that it's important to develop your skill in creating both plot and character. It's simply not enough to be good at one or the other.

In part 1 we built a full-fledged, three-dimensional main character for your story. Creating his or her inner journey has given us 75 percent of our plot, so if you're a character-first novelist who needs to get stronger with plots, you'll need to be sure you've not skipped over part 1. You should like it: We create plot by starting with character.

Now in part 2 we come to the gloriously fun task of creating a plot. The story. If you're a character firster, you may not agree with me yet that creating plot can be as much fun as writing a character's life story or relationship history.

But, what if I were to tell you that plot is simply the stage upon which your characters will perform?

Like a stage, with its furniture and backdrops and intricate lighting setups, the plot is there to perfectly display your characters. It's built around them to give them context and business and set pieces with which to interact as they work out their inner journey. It's there to amplify the themes your main character is exploring. It's there to give structure to their plight and subtext to their decisions.

The plot we're going to build for you will have components that many character-first novelists' stories often lack. Not to put too fine a point on it, but those books are often boring. They lack focus, suspense, direction, or a satisfying sense of closure.

But *Plot Versus Character* will show you how to build a story that has that and more.

Quite simply, you will come up with a better story—more solid and complete and page turning—than any you have ever created before. And it's all to show off your characters. Such a deal.

The centerpiece of part 2 is the three-act structure. Here we create the framework upon which to suspend your main character's inner journey. This is the lens through which we watch and understand your character's arc. We'll also talk about the pros and cons of prologues and how to bring your main characters onstage the first time.

But before we get to any of that, let's talk about the stew your story will simmer in.

12

THE STEW

—————————— ✶ ✶ ✶ ——————— ————

WE COME TO PLOT CREATION AS TO A FRESH WHITE CAN-
vas with a bag full of paints and brushes. This thing can truly be
whatever you want it to be.

Take a minute to dream. For now, don't think about the main
character we've created or his inner journey. Just shut your eyes
and imagine the coolest, most insanely perfect story. Would
it be a torrid romance on the moors of Scotland? A search for
meaning in post-Apocalyptic China? A funny romp through the
aisles of Walmart? An examination of brotherhood on the bat-
tlefields of Afghanistan? A high-flying bank heist story amidst
the moons of Regulon-7?

Just go wacky. If you could write any story about anyone
doing anything, what would it be?

THE KERNEL OF YOUR STORY

Now let's write that book. You have it now, the kernel of the idea
for your novel.

I tricked you, didn't I? Maybe you thought we were just having a fun exercise, a little mental yoga. But I was asking you to find the joyous center of this story. Now we're going to take that delicious story morsel and pair it with your main character's inner journey.

Why not? Just because you've been thinking all along that it would probably be a contemporary romance, it doesn't mean you can't write a pirate story instead. One of the reasons character-first novelists sometimes can't round the corner on good plots is that they're just not interested enough in the one they chose. Throw out the baggage and give yourself permission to write what your heart is telling you the penultimate story would be.

Now, you may not always be able to do this. You may be constrained by an assignment or the ideas of a co-writer. In that case, hit rewind for a bit and do the "what's the ultimate story idea" exercise again, but this time have the broad outline of your story in mind when you do it. It may have to be a contemporary story about the illegal aliens. Okay, what would the ultimate story about illegal aliens be? A thriller? A romance? A murder mystery? You can still go crazy, but you do it within your established parameters.

As we said, your character's inner journey is like a diamond. It's beautiful now, finely chiseled. All it needs is the right setting. But a diamond can fit in a bracelet as well as an engagement ring. It can be on a queen's crown or a cat's collar. A diamond stud could pierce an ear or a belly button with equal beauty. You've got your character's inner journey, but now it's time to choose the setting.

While you consider where to enshrine this treasure, think about the particular beauty of this inner journey. What are the themes and issues involved? What kind of story would best show off or amplify these?

In this chapter we're going to look at elements you might not have considered as part of plot. They'll give rise to ideas for how to better do what it is you're wanting to do with this book.

The first and most important is what I call *the main thing*. It's that ideal novel idea I had you think of a minute ago. When you pair the engaging inner journey you've created for this character with a story kernel that excites you, you're going to have something special on your hands.

So go ahead and imagine it: *This* inner journey set in *that* story. Can it work? How would it work? What story ideas come to you right away? Write them down! These spontaneous sparks will be terrific elements to add to the book.

Keep noodling on this one. Don't be afraid to come back and add more and more brain gems as you unearth them. What would be the coolest way to tell this character's inner journey? Errol Flynn romantic adventure? *Schindler's List* exploration of the depravity of man? *Sneakers*-style high-tech buddy caper? Overland quest? Mistaken identity? Have fun playing with ideas.

For the rest of this chapter we're going to look at aspects of your story's makeup that will color and expand your main character's inner journey, and therefore give substance to your plot. The first is genre.

GENRE

Genre is the sort of novel you're going to write. It's things like western or science fiction or romance or chick-lit. These are publishing categories that align with the fiction interests of large numbers of readers. Romantic comedy, hard-boiled detective, cozy mystery, historical fiction, technothriller, urban fantasy, southern gothic, science fiction, etc. What genre will you pick for this novel?

Maybe your main character's inner journey is someone who is afraid of being an old maid at the end of her life. Now, you could tell that as a contemporary story about a young woman in a ratty apartment in Brooklyn. But what if you told it as a Western about a mail-order bride who arrives in a frontier town only to find out that the man who "ordered" her has died of consumption? Now no one knows or cares about her—and the local outlaws are riding into town.

Or what if you made it a science fiction story about a future in which humans who are unhappy with life can transfer their consciousness into deep space probes that spend eternity journeying across the empty reaches of space? Surely she would consider it—or abhor such a fate.

Do you see how your choice of genre can underline the theme of your main character's inner journey?

So what about your story? What is your main character's primary issue in her inner journey? Hubris? Ambition? Unforgiveness? Fear? Now consider the scores of genres and subgenres out there: Could one of them provide a built-in "speaker system" for amplifying this message?

A little browsing around Amazon.com will turn up more genres than you've likely heard of: everything from sea adventures to family sagas to horror, regency, and space opera.

Your story of a man running from his own self-unforgivness: What if you made it a ghost story? A medical thriller? An epic fantasy? What possibilities present themselves as you consider placing this diamond in those settings?

Your story about a woman trying to climb the corporate ladder so as to never have to rely on anyone: What if the corporate ladder was replaced with a chain of command and she found herself as a woman masquerading as a man in medieval France? What if the reliance she feared became personified in the person of a serial killer on her tail? What if she were Tamar in a biblical novel about Judah, having to disguise herself as a harlot to get his attention?

You don't have to write a genre book. You don't have to put genre—or, really, any of the topics we cover in this chapter—into your novel. We're just looking for ideas, approaches that might intensify your main character's inner journey and thereby give it the impact it deserves.

Don't forget you can combine genres. *Titanic* is a romance and also a historical and a disaster movie. *Firefly* is a science fiction-slash-western series. Blaze a new trail. Invent a new hybrid.

GENRE RAMIFICATIONS

If you do find a genre that seems like a perfect launching pad for the story your character's inner journey tells, take a minute to sketch out what things must be in your book because of your choice.

The reason a genre is a genre is that it's developed a number of conventions and expectations. Readers come to genre novels to find these familiar elements. You are certainly free to create your own version of the genre, but you should at least consider these conventions to see whether they align with the needs of your character's inner journey.

If your main character's inner journey is about his struggle with a fear that he can never live up to his father's expectations, and you've decided to write it as a spy thriller genre novel, see how your choice of genre can help you. The hero will probably be up against an evil mastermind. Is there any way the villain could remind the hero of his own father? Could the hero's superior be a disapproving taskmaster who brings back all those old memories? There will probably be a beautiful woman involved. Well, could she support our hero the way his mother used to? Could the perilous climb to the villain's lair be reminiscent of a climb when the hero spectacularly disappointed his father?

As you go through the list of genres you might choose, think about what each one automatically gives you. A western will give you an isolated, rugged setting, a closeness with horses, a prevalence of men, and a built-in gunfight at high noon. Do any of those resonate with your main character's inner journey? A murder mystery will give you lots of suspicious people with dark motives, many red herrings, an intellectual puzzle, a lurking killer, and a claustrophobic feel for the hero. Do any of those align with what your hero is going through on the inside?

Don't be afraid to consider writing in a genre you've never tried before. If it gives you fabulous ideas for how to strengthen the primary issue under examination, go for it! Remember, everything we're doing in part 2 is finding ways to distill into ever purer form the main character's inner journey. If that means you think it might behoove you to write an Amish romance—or even Amish vampires in space,—just do it!

ERA, SETTING, AND BACKDROP

At what moment in time will you set your novel? Where will you have the story transpire? What will be going on while the character is making his inner journey?

Like genre, the era, setting, and backdrop you choose for your novel can have a tremendous force-multiplication effect on your main character's inner journey.

You may have been thinking you'd set your book in modern-day America, but would it add tools to your kit if you told it in 1890s Ireland instead? What if it were set during the Berlin Olympics in 1936—or in the far future on a research station inside the core of Mercury? Take a minute to cast your eyes about at the different options available to you.

Casablanca could've been set just about anywhere or at any time, but setting it in North Africa during the Nazi regime gave it a flavor and a mystique—not to mention plenty of sinister enemies and a simmering tension—that raised the stakes for the main story.

Let's consider some options.

ERA

When in time do you want your story to happen? In a minute, we'll talk about backdrops—like the Depression, the Revolutionary War, etc. But right now we're just talking about epoch or era, independent of things happening at the time.

If your story took place in the second decade of the 1900s, many things would be different than if it took place in the second decade of the 2000s. Clothing, transportation, communication, health care, science and technology, and more. Now consider if it were taking place in the first decade of the Roman Empire or of Charlemagne's reign.

Let your mind float to other eras for a moment. Would Victorian repression and hypocrisy help you tell your hero's story? Would a futuristic story give you the freedom you need? Would something in prehistoric times echo the savagery of the hero's self-recriminations?

A choice of era can solve story problems for you. Maybe you need the hero to seek a lost civilization, but with today's satellite topography no more pockets for such a thing remain. Setting it even fifty years back would take care of that for you. Maybe you need your character's daughter to be sick with polio or some other disease that modern medicine has all but eradicated. Maybe you need to isolate your character for years at a time—a near-future interplanetary journey might be just the thing.

Playing with *when* you set your story can provide opportunities for your book that you simply wouldn't be able to take advantage of if the book was set in modern times.

So for your story: Would a change of era give you some interesting possibilities? Could your hero's inner journey be drawn in higher relief if you were to use your time machine?

SETTING

Where you set your story can help you accomplish your goals. Without changing the era, a book set in Madagascar is going to be vastly different from one set in Manhattan. Calcutta is not Connecticut. Norway differs greatly from Norman, Oklahoma.

What location have you been envisioning as you've thought of your story? It may be that your first instincts were right on target, but there's no harm in playing with some alternative ideas.

Different locations give you different opportunities and challenges. Pick one that will intensify the theme your hero is dealing with in her inner journey. If she's trying to reclaim a lost childhood, why not set the book in an antique store? If he's trying to avoid having to rely on anyone, why not make him a trapeze artist in a circus? If she's trying to marry a rich man to avoid suffering lack, why not set it on Rodeo Drive—or Skid Row?

Select a location that will automatically color and shape your character's journey. Look for settings that will contrast or reinforce her goal.

The choices here are endless, even if you decide to make it a modern story. A tale set on a farm will be very different from one set on Capitol Hill. And don't limit yourself to broad locations like that; use more specific settings as well: an airplane, an elevator, a cruise ship, a submarine, an underground bunker. A story set in a hot air balloon might underline the helplessness the hero is feeling. A novel set in an amusement park could highlight the joylessness in your hero's heart.

When you add the variable of a different era, your setting options multiply. A ship today would be very different from a ship two hundred years ago. A factory in 2050 would be very different from a factory in 1910. As would a battlefield, a publishing company, or a home.

Explore different ideas for *where* you might set your novel. See if one of them presents some exciting prospects to help show off your hero's arc.

BACKDROP

How would *Gone with the Wind* have been different if it had been set in the 1930s in the midst of Prohibition? The backdrop of the Civil War—and from the Confederacy's point of view, to boot—gave Scarlett's exploits a heightened seriousness. It doesn't hurt that the reader knows history and therefore senses doom in the future for Scarlett and the people she loves.

The Grapes of Wrath would've worked as a story if set against some backdrop other than the Great Depression. But Steinbeck's choice to set it there lends the story a desperation it wouldn't have had if he'd set it in 1950s America during the Cold War.

Backdrop refers to the larger events happening alongside the character's inner journey. These are the looming panoramas—some of them world events, some much more intimate—that frame the story and give it texture.

We Were Soldiers Once ... and Young is set in the Vietnam War. That is its backdrop. *Chariots of Fire* is set against the backdrop of the 1924 Olympics. *Ender's Game* is set against the backdrop of a war against an alien species. The Harry Potter series is set against the return of He Who Shall Not Be Named. *Dear John* is set against the events of 9/11.

Things going on in the world around your main character can help you accomplish your goals. A story about a woman afraid of abandonment would be fine if set in a duplex in Cleveland. But what if you told it as a WWII story and the woman is a Jew in a Nazi concentration camp? Maybe she is thrown in solitary confinement and all but forgotten. Suddenly the prospects of her fears coming true seem much greater, thus deepening her anxieties. A story about a man struggling to be less judgmental would be fine if set in a corporate cubicle—but what if you made him a judge in the Salem witch trials?

You don't have to set the book on the *Lusitania* or in the midst of the war in Iraq—but why not? Why not look for a cultural movement or event that bears some resemblance, either by comparison or contrast, with what your hero is going through on the inside? Very often, just having something like that painted on the back wall of the stage can lend the right aspect to your story. Why *not* use a spice that helps you add an appropriate flavor to your book?

Take a minute to roam through history (or project your thoughts into the future or an alternate world) to see if you might find some backdrop that would enhance your hero's inner journey.

THEME AND MESSAGE

Nobody likes to be preached at in a novel. If you have an agenda, be it global warming or anti-apartheid or conversion to Islam, you're wise to keep it off the front burner in your book.

That's not to imply you can't say something meaningful with your story, of course. The trick is subtlety.

As you think about your main character's inner journey, is there a message at work in the background? If she's trying to deny a repressed part of herself, could your book be saying we must listen to our heart? If he's so bitter he's become less than human, are you maybe implying that unforgivingness is a poison?

Take a look at the old way and the new way duking it out in your hero's inner journey. Chances are, there's a moral here—a lesson the reader can apply in her own life. What you want to do now is consider how you might shrewdly illustrate that truism in your story.

A classic character flaw in literature is selfishness. The hero is so self-absorbed that no one can stand him but himself. Brainstorm ten ways selfishness could be illustrated not in the main character but in the setting and situations around him. This goes back to chapter 10 where I talked about personifying the old way and the new way in the story. Symbolizing your theme is a source of plot ideas that can help you reiterate your hero's conflict *and* give rise to characters and scenes in the book.

Think again about setting and era and backdrop. Even genre. Choices you make there could cause your message to resonate more deeply in the story—and the reader.

TICKING TIME BOMB

Your plot needs suspense. A common complaint about stories written by character-first novelists is that they have very little tension. The (fascinating) characters meander around looking for excuses to have more (wonderful) dialogue. But nothing propels the story forward, which means there is nothing tempting the reader to turn those pages.

You want people "mad" at you for keeping them up all night reading your book. You don't want them telling you your book is a wonderful sedative.

I promised you a plot that would satisfy the reader, would satisfy *you*, and would be a page turner. The first will be accomplished by a solid three-act structure. The second happens when you combine "the main thing" with your main character's inner journey. The third is largely accomplished through what I call the "ticking time bomb."

In fiction, the ticking time bomb is the impending bad thing that will happen if your hero isn't successful in her goal. Sometimes, as in the movie *Speed,* it's a literal bomb. Other times it's a natural disaster like an asteroid hurtling toward Earth or a volcano about to erupt. A sinking ship or an exploding space station. It doesn't have to be huge, though. The ticking time bomb could be the summer ending and the boy moving away or the day of the show coming and they still don't have anyone for the lead role.

What you want is a deadline. Whether it's a fire spreading to the hero's house or a rising tide or an encroaching enemy army, every second that goes by ... it gets closer.

The magic of the time bomb, which you'll establish very early in your book, is that the reader feels the tension increasing with every passing page—even if you don't mention it for several chapters in a row. Sometimes it's even worse for the reader (which is better for the author) if you *don't* mention it, because the reader keeps it alive in her mind. If the characters aren't talking about it, then no one is watching for it, and the reader may appoint herself to the job. Chief Worrier.

If you establish that doom is approaching, your book will have tension. It's as simple and as magical as that.

Maybe the main character knows about the Sword of Damocles hanging over his neck and maybe he doesn't. But the reader knows. It's a delicious anxiety that readers will simultaneously love and hate you for.

James Cameron employed the perfect ticking time bomb by setting a love story on the *Titanic*. Talk about your doomed romances. No matter how high and soaring and fun the early parts of the movie were, we knew catastrophe was coming. It weighed on us. It was excruciatingly delightful to know something the characters didn't know.

Peter Benchley's *Jaws* personifies the ticking time bomb as a killer shark bent on hunting down and killing our heroes. No matter what the characters do, their rendezvous with destiny swims steadily nearer. Michael Ende's *Die Unendliche Geschichte* (which became the film *The Neverending Story* in the United States) depicts a world being overtaken by "the nothing," an all-consuming dark cloud that will, if not halted, destroy everything. Every moment that passes brings that doom closer to catching up with the hero.

Think about your story: its setting and era and backdrop and the main character's inner struggle. What game-ending change can you set up that will force the end of the hero's window of opportunity to accomplish her goal?

Maybe you could set your story in Indonesia in the days just before the 2004 tsunami. Maybe you could set it in the far future just before our sun is about to go supernova. Maybe your hero is a shy middle schooler who has only three more days to talk to that pretty classmate before summer is over and she goes to her father's for three months.

Turn up the heat on your character. Draw a line in the sands of time. Establish a countdown. Raise the stakes. Drop a piano out of the space shuttle and mark the seconds until it lands on … whom?

Every book doesn't need a ticking time bomb. The Dark Lord isn't always about to destroy the free world. War isn't always about to sweep the continent. Sometimes the asteroid misses the earth—or there never was an asteroid. And of course there are many other ways to create suspense in a novel besides impending doom.

But why wouldn't you want to add the power of this tension-creating automaton to your novel? Tell me again why you wouldn't want your book to be a page turner.

Take ten minutes to let your mind explore possibilities for some kind of dire countdown you could set to ticking in your story. Maybe there aren't any (though I doubt it). And maybe you decide not to use it even if you think of a good one. But winding up a clock on a bomb and setting it at the base of your character's life is a great way to ratchet up the tension, suggest ideas for your plot, and keep the reader up late at night.

THE VILLAIN

The last ingredient in our preplot stew is your book's antagonist. If fiction is about someone who wants something, then there must be an obstacle in his way. If the hero wants to become president and he does, you have no story. Better said, fiction is about someone who wants something despite the fact that something or someone stands in his way. Fiction is conflict.

Before we get into your book's three-act structure, let's spend a minute thinking about a villain.

On one level, your novel is about a bad guy trying to do a bad thing. This is true even if you have no personified villain—you've still got an OR-ELSE thing that will happen if the hero can't achieve victory. When it comes to the external story of your book, you need to know what is going on in the book, who is doing it, and why. What is the bad thing that someone is trying to do in your story, and who is doing it?

If you're writing a suspense thriller or a mystery or a horror novel, you already know there has to be a bad guy. There simply would be no tale to tell without one. But if you're writing a romantic comedy or a multigenerational women's relationship novel, you may not automatically feel the need for a black hat.

Not so fast. The antagonist doesn't have to be a villain, per se, and it doesn't even need to be a person. *Music Within* is about one man's fight against prejudice, a fight that resulted in the Americans with Disabilities Act. *Robinson Crusoe* has the occasional enemy to run off, but most of the time his nemesis is simply his isolation. Social status limitations could be a hero's enemy. A physical disfigurement or illness could stand in the character's way of achieving his goals. A best friend who is dating the boy the hero wants to date is not necessarily a villain, but she's certainly an obstacle.

Whether or not you want to have a spindly legged villain twirling his mustache, you do need to set something in your hero's way. So think about your story. What could be the primary obstacle in the way of what your main character wants?

If you've built a character all the way through part 1, you may have the answer built in. Your villain could be that person, group, creature, or force that represents the new way. Or even the old way.

Phil Connors just wants to get back to his career and selfish life, but he is blocked from doing so by the time warp he finds himself in. Fitzcarraldo wants to get a steamboat across a mountain, but the sheer difficulty of the endeavor seeks to thwart him. The freak outbreak of tornados in *Twister* seems out to get the heroes.

The common denominator in stories like those is that the villain is really an ally in disguise. Each of these forces comes against the character, but not to harm him. Rather, the character is out of kilter and the apparent villain is actually a corrective force. Novel-length tough love. The aim is to break the hero of his harmful way and steer him into the light.

With your story, would it work to play it out like this? Could the antagonist really be on the hero's side? Or if not on his side, exactly, then perhaps the villain could be something that Fate uses to teach the hero his lesson?

Most stories are best served with a traditional antagonist. This is the classic man versus man kind of story: the two gunslingers facing off in front of the saloon; the hero who has quested across the realm entering the monster's lair to "end this once and for all"; the detective finally catching up with the killer; the showdown in the exploding undersea base.

Think about your story. What kind of villain could you create that would be the best choice to bring about the hero's inner conflict?

If your hero is struggling to retain her decency in the face of a crumbling moral center, your villain might be what the hero could become if she gave in and went that way. If your hero can't forgive himself for a mistake that cost the life of a child, maybe the villain is attempting to wipe out an entire pediatric hospital with a biological weapon. Find a way to use the antagonist to bring out some key aspect of the hero's inner journey.

If a man versus man story doesn't work for you, look to the other possibilities: man versus nature (*Jaws, The Perfect Storm*), man versus self (*The Strange Case of Dr. Jekyll and Mr. Hyde*), man versus technology (*Do Androids Dream of Electric Sheep?, Terminator*), man versus society (*Pride & Prejudice,*), man versus the supernatural or Fate (*Oedipus Rex, Matrix, Groundhog Day*).

Your book has to be about conflict or there is no story. Something or someone has to stand in the way of your hero or it's not a novel, it's a slice-of-life essay. A long blog entry.

Make the thing blocking your hero's path strong. It has to be a worthy adversary. Your hero is only as heroic as the strength of the villain she overcomes. If your antagonist is the literary equivalent of a lawn gnome, your hero doesn't seem exactly epic when she prevails. But if you turn the lawn gnome into a towering metal golem aflame with the souls of the undead, you've got yourself a story.

Who or what will the villain be for your novel?

SIMMER AND SERVE

I hope this chapter has prompted you to take out your legal pad or laptop to jot down your thoughts. My goal has been to throw TruGreen on the rich soil of your mind to give rise to a hundred ideas that might go into your story. We haven't yet gotten to building your plot, precisely, but I want your mind brimming with possibilities.

In theatrical terms, we're dressing the set. We're building props and sewing costumes. We're choosing drops and setting up lights. We already know who our actors are and what parts they're going to play. Now we're having fun figuring out how it's all going to look.

By examining multiple options for genre, era, villain, and the rest, we're experimenting with how to best present this amazing internal journey the main character will go on. If *Romeo and Juliet* can work just as well as *West Side Story* and *A Christmas Carol* can become *Ghosts of Girlfriends Past*, maybe your story could produce a whole set of fresh possibilities when you have a little fun trying out options beyond the ones that occurred to you originally.

As we begin hammering out the plot of your book, come back to these variables often. Don't be afraid to turn your heroic fantasy into a comedy of errors if that helps you better showcase your hero's inner journey.

13

OF PROLOGUES AND INTRODUCTIONS

* * *

YOU DON'T KNOW ABOUT ME WITHOUT YOU have read a book by the name of *The Adventures of Tom Sawyer;* but that ain't no matter. That book was made by Mr. Mark Twain, and he told the truth, mainly. There was things which he stretched, but mainly he told the truth. That is nothing. I never seen anybody but lied one time or another, without it was Aunt Polly, or the widow, or maybe Mary. Aunt Polly—Tom's Aunt Polly, she is—and Mary, and the Widow Douglas is all told about in that book, which is mostly a true book, with some stretchers, as I said before.
—**Mark Twain,** *The Adventures of Huckleberry Finn*

How will you begin your novel? A splendid first line, I hope, and an immediate grabber to engage the reader. Will you begin with a prologue or just get right into the main action of the book? Will you start with your protagonist onstage or will you show other characters first?

When you teach novelists in the writers' conference setting, as I do, you hear what other people are teaching them, especially when it conflicts with what *you've* been teaching. The attendees come up to you and say, "How come you say to do X when the guy next door is saying to do Y?" There are few topics in fiction craftsmanship parlance that are more controversial, it seems, than how to begin your book.

In this chapter I'm going to talk about the opening pages of your novel. At first this may seem like a deviation from either plot or character, but it is not. There are certain things you should do at the outset to introduce key *characters* correctly so as to get your *plot* going well.

TO PROLOGUE OR NOT TO PROLOGUE

A prologue is a scene or section that precedes the main action of your novel. Sometimes it involves action that will be covered in the pages of the current book. Other times it recounts something that happened outside the story proper, as with an event that happened long before the current story begins. Sometimes it's a scene that happens later in the story chronology—a flash-forward—and the rest of the story is catching us up to that moment.

Are prologues good, bad, or neutral? Better question: Should *your* novel have a prologue? If you listen to some fiction teachers, they will tell you that prologues are evil and must be destroyed.

I watch agents and editors as they look over unpublished writers' proposals, often in the writers' conference setting. When some of these folks turn to the sample chapters and see a prologue, I have seen them rip out those pages and toss them aside.

Seriously. It's insane. It's as if a book is wrongly written simply if the first page has the word Prologue written across the top. In my mind, that's like throwing out every book whose first sentence uses some arbitrary word that the editor doesn't like such as *eggplant* or *computer*.

Google "fiction prologues" and you'll find dozens of blog entries and articles about why prologues don't work and why you should never use them.

Hogswallop.

Now, to be fair, many novelists do prologues poorly and for the wrong reasons. The primary misuse of a prologue is to dump a ton of backstory on the reader so the author feels free to go ahead and start the story. "Whew, glad I got all that out of the way." In that case, the prologue should be removed entirely.

Other reasons to discard a prologue include when the style or tone of the prologue is unlike anything else in the book, when it's a flash-forward from the book and is included just to grab the reader, and when the prologue presents information that is laid out sufficiently elsewhere.

In cases like this, I agree that the prologue is a problem. However, the proper conclusion isn't that all prologues are bad, just that *these* prologues are bad. If you can write a prologue that doesn't go wrong, it can be a beautiful thing for your book.

Here's the bizarre thing: Those same agents and editors sometimes accept this same material if the author simply edits "Prologue" from the top of the page and types in "Chapter 1" instead. Craziness.

Anyone who rejects a book simply because it has a prologue is akin to someone swearing off bananas because some of them are overripe. The answer isn't to avoid all bananas but to be careful about which ones to eat.

As I mentioned in part 1, I'm a big believer in establishing normal before you violate normal. It's important to show what a character's life is like before the main story intrudes. Otherwise, we simply can't tell (and don't care) that her life, which we haven't seen, has been turned upside down.

But these "normal" scenes are, by definition, usually more concerned with introducing the main character in her typical life than about getting the story off to a rollicking start. It's possible to do both with an opening scene, but not always desirable. How much better for everyone if, before we do a slice-of-life scene, we've already gotten the reader engaged and have started the time bomb ticking down? Then you can take a minute to show the character's normal life without losing momentum.

Consider the animated film *Mulan*. The first time we meet the central character she's … feeding chickens. Woo-hoo. It's a funny scene and very quickly gets to some terrific music, but it's pretty bucolic, and even then it's about her appointment not with destiny but with the matchmaker. It would've been a pretty boring way to begin the story—had we not already seen what amounts to a prologue: the enemy general Shan-Yu and his army swarming across the Great Wall of China and launching an invasion.

Now when we cut to Mulan feeding chickens, it's tinged with danger. An enemy is coming! Doesn't she know? As she's going about the business of getting dolled up to meet the matchmaker, we're feeling the inexorable approach of Bad Things.

The prologue works because it establishes the villain, the danger, and the countdown to doom. Though the introduction scene for this young woman is not in itself action oriented, we don't mind. It's entertaining in its own right and it shows who this person is. Best of all, it sets up a nice juxtaposition between villain and hero. The story has linked these two, though they themselves don't know they're on a collision course for one another. And the introductory scene for the hero didn't have to also bear the burden of engaging the reader with action. A great prologue took care of that.

Think about your book. As you read the section in the previous chapter about the time bomb, did you come up with something excellent? Would it work as the opening of your book? In order for a time bomb to be an effective device to generate increasing suspense throughout the story, it has to be introduced early in the book. Why not on page 1?

Of course, you do want to make the main character's introductory scene fascinating. We'll talk about that in a sec. But if you've already gotten the suspense going, that's one less thing the introductory scene has to take care of.

WHAT MAKES A GOOD PROLOGUE

If you decide that a prologue makes sense for your novel, then make sure your prologue sets exactly the right tone. If this is going to be a thriller, a thrilling prologue is what you're after. If it's to be a journey of wondrous discovery, then begin it with something bizarre. If it's going to be a sweet romance, begin it sweetly. The first crucial element for a prologue is that it give your book the perfect flavor.

A good prologue will also establish suspense, as we've said. The stakes are hinted at (if not made explicit). The time bomb will be set to ticking. The volcano is rumbling. The asteroid is buffeted by a solar flare and turns ever so slightly so that Earth is now in its crosshairs. Cracks no one else sees form in the base of the dam. Uproar will ensue.

Ideally, your prologue will also introduce your antagonist. There she is, up to no good. In some genres it's best to keep the *identity* of the bad guy hidden, but a prologue can still introduce the *presence* of a bad guy. Knowing that someone's lurking out there will add tension.

The perfect prologue:

- Sets the right mood for your book
- Establishes the danger or stakes
- Starts the timer ticking down
- Introduces the villain

Some anti-prologuers object to prologues that "do nothing but introduce the bad guy and start the book off with a bang." Certainly if the prologue has no bearing on the story or is of a style completely different from the rest of the book, it's probably best jettisoned. But if your prologue has started the book off with a bang and introduced the villain, I say it's a win.

Though I've hinted at it, it bears explicit mention that certain things ought *not* go in a prologue:

- *Backstory*—If you're suffering from the inability to resist explaining what happened before your story began, seek professional help. Seriously. No place in your book will benefit from your stopping the momentum to indulge your compulsion to get your character histories on the table. There is a place for filling the reader in (a mission briefing scene, for instance), but it is never in the opening pages of your book. Keep the histories, explanations, and other forms of telling (including most flashbacks) out of your prologue.

- *Off-Tone Content*—If your novel is about the many adventures of a puppy named Snuggles, don't start your book with a prologue about nuclear war. Okay, maybe that's an extreme example (*A Boy and His Dog* notwithstanding), but the point is that you need to be sure your prologue sets the right tone for the book that's going to come after it.

- *Random Action Scene*—Whether it's an exciting scene from later in the story or a scene with no purpose other than to start off with a pow, random action scenes are a bad way to start a book.

Not every book will need a prologue. Many of the books that have them would do just as well—or better—without them. However, if done well and for the right reasons, a prologue can significantly help a book. Consider how your book might be changed if you showed your antagonist setting up the challenge for the hero. Go over all the arguments for and against prologues and think about how those points relate to your own novel—and then decide if a prologue will work for you.

BRINGING YOUR MAIN CHARACTER ONSTAGE FOR THE FIRST TIME

Many novelists give little thought to how they're going to lift the curtain on their main character. They begin with the character in a conversation or doing something uncharacteristic of him. Often this is because they're trying to engage the reader with action while also introducing the main character.

In fiction, as in life, first impressions are crucial. The first time the reader sees your protagonist, you want her doing the perfect thing, something that instantly typifies her and shows what's wonderful about her.

Remember that character monologue scene you created back in chapter 8? I mentioned we'd be using that again. Now's the time. Take a look at that scene you wrote, the one that shows off your hero in his ultimate setting, doing and talking about the things that reveal the essence of his character. That may have been a hypothetical dream scene when you wrote it in part 1, but in part 2 it's time to put it to work in the real world, i.e., the real world of your story.

If you could introduce your main character in the perfect way—given the genre, setting, era, etc., of *this* book—how would you do it? The soliloquy you wrote in chapter 8 is the perfect resource for this scene. Go back and look at the elements you identified then that differentiate your character from every other character, and consider how you can bring those out in a scene in this book.

It's no mistake that every James Bond film begins with 007 doing something incredible to take down the bad guys or get the information he needs. There's usually a beautiful woman involved in the event as well. We get a perfect sense of who this character is (and what kind of story this is going to be) before anything else has happened.

That's what we're going for with your book. So let your mind hover over your character and your "story stew" a bit and think about ways you could reveal her essence in an introductory scene.

The best example I know of a great character introduction is the opening sequence from the movie *Raiders of the Lost Ark*. Remember the iconic jungle scenes? With very few words uttered, we get to see exactly what this Indiana Jones person is like. We see that he's a tough hombre who knows his way around not only a gun but a whip. We learn he knows a lot about ancient traps and treasures. We see his grit and daring. We feel like he could punch our lights out. We see his resourcefulness. We also see his limits, his vanity (the hat), and a taste for his fears (the snake). We even meet his nemesis.

By the end of that sequence, when he's swinging through the trees and flying away in the get-away plane, we know not only who this person is but what kind of movie this is going to be.

If it had to, this sequence could stand alone as a short film. It is a self-contained unit in and of itself, with a great story arc. The fact that it's the beginning of the movie sets the viewers' expectations. They know it's going to be a very special ride.

To bring your main character onstage the first time, write a short story. Pretend this is a cameo, the only time she's going to be in the story, but you want to give her an unforgettable moment of glory.

Begin with what you have identified as the essence, the core, of this person, and craft an episode around that. Keep your character's soliloquy in mind, as well as the Indiana Jones and James Bond examples, and see what you can come up with.

Of course it doesn't have to be an action scene. If your story is a romantic comedy, an action scene would be all wrong. Remember Mulan and the chickens. Just think about what kind of book this is going to be and write a fun little scene or sequence that allows your main character to reveal who she is at heart.

This introduction is the perfect opportunity to reveal what your character is wanting or trying to achieve *and* what's likable about her. Your reader is thinking of committing days or even months to your book, and if she's going to spend three hundred-plus pages with this character, she'd better not be a jerk. Even if she *is* a jerk and that's the whole point of her inner journey (eradicating her unpleasantness), you still have to show us something sympathetic about her in these opening moments.

Your protagonist isn't the only character you should craft a special introduction for. If you have an antagonist, that person ought to have a wonderful intro too—perhaps in the prologue. If there is a romantic interest in your book, that person should be brought on with a carefully crafted scene to give us—and the main character—the right first impression. Sidekicks, henchmen, possible suspects, and anyone else you want to feature should get his or her own well-chosen walk-on scene.

Lesser characters should get less-developed introductory scenes, of course. Maybe it's just a moment, like a character stumbling into a room and dropping a box of doughnuts or a fabulous quick scene of a singing telegram at the door. Who can forget Dickens' introduction in *A Tale of Two Cities* to Marquis Evrémonde, who runs down a plebian child in his carriage and then curses peasants for getting in his way?

Barliman Butterburr has a small part in *The Lord of the Rings*, but it's memorable. The first time we see him he's doing exactly what he does: tending to his tavern guests. But he's kind and affable, and Tolkien created a scene that revealed Butterburr's chief characteristics, and his forgetfulness, which becomes important later.

Use that model as you're constructing introductory scenes for your featured minor characters. Give thought to how you can raise the curtain on them in their essence and doing what characterizes them.

As we come to the end of this chapter, I'd like to spend a minute on the topic of the prologue-free novel. A story that doesn't begin with a prologue still needs to begin well, right? It still needs to engage the reader and get the energy flowing. If you choose to go sans prologue, your opening scene will need to do triple duty. Not only do you need to kick off the book in a way that gives the story the right tone, you also need to introduce the main character (because any opening scene that doesn't introduce the main character is a prologue!). So you have to find a method for giving the hero the perfect entrance *and* engage the reader *and* set the right flavor for the book.

It can be done, certainly, and done well. The James Bond and Indiana Jones movies do it every time. Go for it.

PRELIMINARIES COMPLETE

We've covered a lot of territory for your plot and we haven't even discussed three-act structure yet. You know the genre and backdrop of your story. You've developed your villain and the ultimate fun thing you want to do with this book. You've considered era and setting and theme and the ramifications thereof. Now you've planned how your book begins and how you will bring your hero onstage the first time.

Your story's stew is filled with spices and flavors that will affect not only the story to come but the reader's experience of it. If I've done my job right, your mind is brimming with ideas for elements you want to include in your story—and we haven't even started talking about structure. See how tricky I am? It's my aim to get you excited about something you've always thought you were no good at.

Now let's continue the fun and plan out your novel.

14

UNDERSTANDING THREE-ACT STRUCTURE

* * *

LIFE IS A MODERATELY GOOD PLAY WITH A badly written third act.

—Truman Capote

Now we move to the structure of your plot. Everything we've done so far in part 2 has been to prepare for this, because here is where we actually build the framework for your novel. The genre, theme, era, villain, and the rest will inform and color what we do now, but this is the main work. It's like deciding whether to build a speedboat or a fishing boat: Function and design will vary, but certain structural principles will be the same no matter what.

There are as many definitions of what three-act structure is as there are definers. Experts differ on what the acts are, what they do, and where they divide. Some even say three-act structure is woefully outdated, or that novels that use it are formulaic.

If you find a structure that helps you tell your story and accomplish your goal, it's a win, in my opinion. Whether it has three acts or five or twenty, who's to know or mind? However, for those character-first novelists or anyone else hoping to seize upon a framework that makes readers breathlessly turn pages and leaves them feeling satisfied at the end, there's nothing wrong and everything right about working with the classic structure developed by storytellers across the millennia.

Essentially, three-act structure is a way of organizing your story. The simplest way to explain it is "beginning, middle, and end." I've also heard the three acts defined as river, rapids, and waterfall. That's helpful to understand the increasing drama and speed of the story as it moves along. You may also have heard the acts described as setup, confrontation, and resolution. That description gets a little closer to how I see it but draws the line in the wrong place, in my opinion.

For our purposes, we're going to use these terms:

- Act 1: Introductions
- Act 2: The Heart of the Matter
- Act 3: Climax and Dénouement

And, as usual, I'm going to talk about them out of order. Explaining the heart of it first helps the other parts make sense, in my opinion. I'll start with Act 2, then move to Act 1, and finally to Act 3.

THREE-ACT STRUCTURE AT A GLANCE

I've created a new graphic for Part 2. Here it is at its simplest:

Introduction	The Heart of the Matter	Climax & Dénouement
ACT 1	ACT 2	ACT 3

As we'll see in the next chapter, the heart of your story is Act 2. It's where the defining actions of the plot and your main character's inner journey take place.

But you can't just start right there. You can't start with Frodo already on his quest to Mount Doom or none of it will make sense—and the reader won't care. You have to set up what's going on, who these people are, what the stakes are, who the bad guy is, and why it's all important. Those introductions are the stuff of Act 1.

When the conflicts of Act 2 come to a head, you're in Act 3 territory. Here, you show the final confrontation between the hero and his chief adversary. Act 3 also includes the dénouement or "falling action," the fallout and tying off that constitute the end of a novel.

In terms of story movement, we've already talked about river, rapids, and waterfall. That shows the speed and danger of the story's progression. But it doesn't capture the feeling of heightened drama well enough for me. How about a graphical map of the three acts:

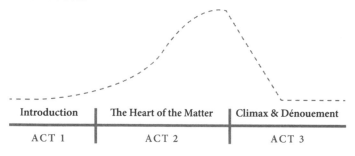

Introduction	The Heart of the Matter	Climax & Dénouement
ACT 1	ACT 2	ACT 3

Everything rises to that diving board at the top—and the stuntman drop pad at the bottom. Maybe it's not a diving board. Maybe it's a yard high above the deck of the *Hispaniola*. And depending on what happens in the climactic moment, the pit of pillows might become a pit of acid.

You can see that Act 1 is where we start to get acquainted with the situation and the characters. Act 2, is, as the title suggests, is the heart of the matter. Everything but the big finish happens in Act 2. How we get from the hero in his resting state to the hero taking a flying leap off the diving board is what we're interested in as readers.

WHO NEEDS A PLOT?

Silly question, right? But think about it for a minute. Why do we need one?

The core of any novel built with *Plot Versus Character* is the main character's inner journey. It is, in essence, a psychological quest, a movement toward—or away from—transformation. That's what the real story is. But this is largely invisible. Internal. Because we always want to show and not tell, and because we don't want a novel that is nothing more than a stream of consciousness monologue, we seek to play that out somehow with characters, settings, and scenes. We want a story, something that could be depicted onstage. Or, we always hope, made into a movie.

The trick is to make visible that which is invisible. To externalize that which is internal. To incarnate a spiritual truth into a physical, observable form.

That's what your plot is. It's the "body host" for the ephemeral truism of a character in transition. It's also the thing that makes it interesting to watch your story unfold.

Just as words are the vehicles for ideas, so a plot is the vehicle for your protagonist's transformation. Without words, no one would be able to comprehend your amazing revelation. Without a plot, no one would be able to experience the meaning of your character's journey to change. The more articulate a speaker, the better his original concept can cross the void and reconstruct itself in your mind in a form as close as possible to what it was in the speaker's mind.

An artist may have an idea for an image or song. It may be fully formed in her mind's eye. But until she can translate it into some observable form—painting, sculpture, song—it remains trapped and unexpressed. So it is with plot. Your novel's plot is the form you give to this incredible internal conflict and resolution you have in mind. It is the way we detect and internalize the idea you want to express.

So let's start getting this marvelous story out of your mind and into reality.

15

ACT 2: THE HEART OF THE MATTER

* * *

YOUR STORY IS ALL ABOUT THE MIDDLE.

In part 1 we talked about how the escalation phase of the character's inner journey is the core of her story. That makes it the core of *the* story. The escalation phase is roughly analogous to Act 2 of your plot.

In her inner journey, the escalation is where the old way and the new way are fighting it out. The old, hurtful method she's decided is best for her has encountered a true challenger in this persistent new way. Like Phil Connors trying to escape his recurring Groundhog Day or Ebenezer Scrooge trying to get away from his ghosts, every effort to get back to the way things were is thwarted. She's getting more and more desperate as she nears the end of herself.

That's what is playing out in Act 2 of the plot. In other words, Act 2 is the place that provides the space for this crucial interplay in the hero's psyche.

You do that by providing *conflict*. Conflict makes us angry. It causes our emotions to rise. It brings out the worst and best in us. It drives to the surface those things we'd been harboring in secret. In short, it externalizes that which would otherwise remain internalized and hidden.

FUN IN THE MIDDLE

As I said about the escalation phase for your character's inner journey, on the plot side, Act 2 is the fun of your book. The other acts are there as support for Act 2. Act 1 is the setup you'll need to begin the fun, and Act 3 culminates the fun with a ta-da!

Consider our three-act structure diagram in light of William Golding's *The Lord of the Flies*.

Introduction	The Heart of the Matter	Climax & Dénouement
ACT 1	ACT 2	ACT 3

The delicious part of this book is the middle, the growing strife between Jack and Ralph. Act 2 is the whole downward spiral of the group from refined British schoolboys to murderous jungle creatures. Here Golding gives us tremendous character studies and an exploration of group dynamics and the devolution of morality.

The "fun" of this story is that descent, but Golding couldn't have started the book right then. First we had to meet everybody. First we had to see the situation. Certain things had to be set up before the heart of the story could begin: that they had crashed here, that they were proper English schoolboys, that they were hoping to get rescued immediately, and that they were really on a deserted island. That was what Golding did in Act 1.

On the other end, the conflict between Ralph's boys and Jack's hunters (shown in fascinating detail in Act 2) built to the climactic meeting in which Piggy is killed. That climax and the rest of the descent into savagery constitutes Act 3.

Do you see how Act 2 is where most of the action happens? Act 1 sets it up and Act 3 takes it to its logical conclusion.

ACT 2 IN YOUR NOVEL

All right, we've been speaking theoretically for a while now. It's time to get back to your novel. Let's think about what three-act structure we can give it.

Look back over your notes on your main character's escalation phase in her inner journey. That's the core of the book. It's the thing we're going to depict not only in Act 2 but in Acts 1 and 3 as well. Refresh your memory about what "new way" she's trying to quickly overcome and what "old way" she's trying to get back to. Get a firm handle again on her knot and the alternative the story offers.

Then think of how to depict that externally.

You've already considered characters who could symbolize the old and new ways, so begin your thinking there. Did you come up with some great ideas? What about elements from the backdrop or genre or setting of your book? The villain? The "main thing"? Gather up all those preliminaries and array them before you so you can look at them at once and begin to synthesize.

The original *Star Wars* movie (my favorite movie of all time, I should point out) has a good three-act structure. Examining it will help us understand the three acts and, I hope, give you what you need to determine those acts for your book.

There are many ways to dissect this film, but here's how I do it. In my mind, Act 2 is the entire sequence in which our heroes are inside the Death Star. In this sequence, the heroes meet great danger, encounter many setbacks, overcome obstacles, pull off a caper, rescue a princess, gel as a team, and accomplish their escape. Those are the external plot trappings. They're a kick to watch.

But the most important thing that's happening is that our primary hero is coming of age.

Luke Skywalker started out the movie as a spoiled teenager trying to get out of work on the family farm. At the climax of the movie (in Act 3) he's a levelheaded young man willing to give his life for a cause he believes in. What happened? What brought about such a change?

Why, Act 2 happened, of course. During that time in the Death Star, Luke matured a great deal. He discovered he was strong. He lived through battle. He defied an empire. He rescued a princess. He became a hero in deed, not just word. He did something no one else could do or had even tried to do. He also suffered a great loss, which compounded the losses he'd already endured since the story began. In a very short time, he grew up.

Do you see how the events of the plot provided the sculpting he needed? What was really happening was something invisible, on the inside, but these changes were triggered by very visible enemies and events. How he *acted* on the outside over the course of the story revealed how he'd *changed* on the inside.

So it should be with your novel.

FORGIVE THE INTRUSION

Think about your main character's inner journey. What external events could you bring in that would trigger the changes and the conflict you're wanting for your hero?

We've already thought about the inciting incident. Remind yourself of that moment when the new way invaded your hero's life and started him on this detour that will lead to his transformation. Now extrapolate from there. How can things escalate? I don't mean an escalation in the inside of the character, though that is certainly happening at the same time, but on the outside.

To disambiguate the inciting incident in the character's inner journey from the inciting incident in the external plot, I call the latter the *intrusion.*

The intrusion is that moment when the main action of the story invades the hero's life. In *The Hurt Locker* the hero's life is invaded when he believes an Iraqi child he's befriended has been murdered. The main story begins when this event intrudes into his sphere.

It can be confusing, I know, because many times the inciting event in the main character's life is also the intrusion. When Lightning McQueen gets diverted to Radiator Springs, it's the beginning of the external action and his inner journey. But it's important to think of the two as separate because sometimes they are.

I wrote a novel about an emergency room physician who gets caught up in a mystery involving the abortion industry in his city. The intrusion was when he had to sign both a birth certificate and a death certificate of a baby who had (briefly) survived a botched abortion. But his inner journey had to do with self-acceptance, and that arc didn't begin until he saw someone giving genuine, condition-free love to an "undeserving" person. That first example of acceptance was the thing that got him thinking.

In your story, think about whether your character's inciting event and the story's intrusion are the same event or different. That will help you stay disambiguated as you write.

If the intrusion was the arrival of an annoying relative from out of town, could that character decide to move in with the hero? Could that initial irritation become a source of more irritation as the story progresses? If the intrusion is the attack on Pearl Harbor, could the hero plunge into the war effort in the Pacific for the rest of the book? If the intrusion is an invasion by aliens, could the hero vow to fight them until his last breath?

If Jacob Marley's arrival constitutes Scrooge's intrusion, could Marley or other ghosts press that interruption throughout the course of the story? (Of course that's what Dickens does.) If the intrusion is Romeo meeting Juliet for the first time, could the desire to see Juliet—and all the perils involved therein—provide a stream of conflict for the story?

What you're looking for is a plentiful source of external conflict to power the main part of your book.

Not just any conflict. Not random conflict. But conflict perfectly tailored to aggravate your hero's knot. Your hero has embraced a way of living that is hurting him, whether he realizes it or not. It is your job to design a special kind of assault to beat it out of him.

What external attack or aggravation could you bring into your hero's life that would unerringly get at that dysfunction in his life?

If his knot is an unforgivingness that drives him to isolation, can you surround him with happy houseguests who won't take a hint? If her knot is selfishness, can you drop into her life some needy people whom no one else will help? If his knot is a fear of abandonment, can you plop him alone onto a deserted island or get him thrown into solitary confinement? If her knot is hubris, can you entrap her in a job that will systematically humiliate her?

If you could design the perfect foil for your hero's "sin," what would it be?

Look for not just one event but a rich source of ongoing conflict, a force that will continue to apply ever-increasing opposition to his efforts to go back to the old way.

Phil Connors simply couldn't escape the time warp he was in. The more he tried, the harder he fell. Ralph simply could not get Jack and the rest of the boys to behave civilly the longer they remained marooned on the island. Scrooge simply could not make the ghostly visitations stop.

It doesn't have to be a conflict leading to bloodshed or misery. The only thing that's important is that the character's desire to go back to his semi-happy dysfunction of before is continually thwarted.

In the movie *Just Like Heaven,* a man with unresolved grief over a loss moves into an apartment—and is confronted by the former tenant. Except she's supposed to be dead and she keeps walking through tables. He wants her to go away but she won't. In one classic scene, he's trying to watch television and she's lying on the coffee table in front of him belting out "The sun'll come out tomorrow!" from *Annie.* No matter what he tries, he can't get rid of her. It's a wonderful source of ongoing conflict that ultimately causes both characters to deal with their issues.

In *The Game Plan,* the sudden appearance of Joe Kingman's daughter on his stoop interrupts his rich bachelor life. But it is her continued presence that repeatedly gets in the way of his preferred lifestyle. That lifestyle was poisonous, but he couldn't see it. His little girl represents the antidote, but he can't see that either. Slowly, with each step triggered by external events, her gentle influence begins to reach into his narcissism. He begins to realize that she needs him—and, ultimately, that he needs her.

If this irritant had never entered his life, he never would've been transformed for the better.

How do you want to irritate your hero?

BUILDING THE FRAMEWORK

When you know the source of conflict that is going to vex your hero, you're ready to build the framework for Act 2. You're ready to lay the first tracks for what will become the cross-country railroad of your story. We'll start in the middle and extend forward and backward until the whole line is connected.

So sit back and think of how you can arrange a series of misfortunes for your poor hero. You know what her knot is and what the alternative is going to be. You've now come up with the source of conflict that will, like a perfectly designed surgical tool, begin to dig into her until it gets at the tumor. Try not to cackle like a supervillain, okay?

Brainstorm six or ten ways this source of conflict can begin the beat-down of your hero. Arrange them from least serious to most serious.

Now jot down ideas for how she might respond to each one, always trying to be rid of the problem to get back to her old way. How will she react to this campaign launched upon her? Go back to your notes about her core character. Reread her soliloquy. If this particular source of conflict came upon her, what would she do? What creative ways would she try to overcome it? When each one failed, how would she escalate? Trace out an idea or six of how she might spiral upward in frustration and anxiety—especially as the time bomb ticks closer and closer to zero.

How would she respond if things got even more desperate? What would she do if all else failed? What extreme measures would she be willing to take now that things are deadly serious? Here's where you're getting near her core. You've drilled down to the final barrier and are near a breakthrough. The character herself will feel that things are crumbling around her, but you know she's almost reached the point where good things will be only a choice away.

Now, keep in mind that what you're mainly working on here are *external plot escalations*. It feels like inner journey stuff, I know, and if you want to you can brainstorm some more good escalation ideas now. But what you really need to produce here are ways the external story can get more and more serious. Think about your villain—what's he up to now? How is he making things intolerable?

Think about the OR-ELSE ramifications if the hero doesn't stop him. How can those be made to look more serious or likely?

Arrange all these ideas into a rough event map. As you read it on paper or on the screen, it should resemble a list of rising actions that describe an escalating conflict. Begin with the inciting incident and write down an external event that will cause your hero to be frustrated in getting back to his old way. Then put down what he'll do to get past that. Next will be the new, more serious attack, followed by his escalated response. And so it should go, always mounting, until the hero is beside himself with anxiety and frustration.

Jot down notes along the way to show where she is in the transformation process. Comments like "still in denial," "starting to crack," or "beginning to reconsider his life" can help you map her progress toward her moment of truth even while thinking about external plot events.

You might also include a separate column that tracks the progress of the ticking time bomb. The hero's desperation rises right alongside the increasing danger, giving you one frenetic Act 2. Because you've just mapped out your Act 2. (I tricked you again!)

The middle act is escalating conflict. Through this central section of your novel, your character's defenses are overcome one by one. It's the beat-down in full swing. Externally, it may be a story about a soccer team or a battle or a forbidden romance, but it's really about your hero.

And that's the framework for Act 2.

GOING FROM MAP TO MANUSCRIPT

You'll need to flesh out that map you've come up with. Perhaps the external plot involves the hero dealing with an invasion of fire ants in his dream home property. Maybe you've decided that the second escalation is that the ant infestation has somehow beaten the insecticide your hero laid out, and the third escalation has the ants eating the wiring inside the house, and you have no idea how to get from point to point. That's okay. Either you can figure it all out now or you can save the real discovery for the writing process.

When I write, I like to have my landmarks circled on the map, so to speak, but I like waiting until I'm doing the actual writing to figure out how to get from one to the next.

You aren't bound by this map you've made. Once you sit down to write it, you may discover that it works better to switch the order of some of the items or you may come up with even better ideas later. That's fine. So long as you remember that this is an escalation of conflict designed to draw out (or beat out) your hero's knot, you'll be in good shape.

I hope you can see the significance of what you've just done. You now have a rough outline of the core of your book. You'll have fun stringing together these incidents into a cohesive progression, I'm sure. You can do so resting in the knowledge that this will be a satisfying, page-turning middle segment and that it is accomplishing your goals for illuminating the character's inner journey.

In one sense, we're just getting started with your plot. But in another, you're almost done. The hard part is over.

For Act I, you'll simply get down on paper the setup necessary to get you into Act 2. And Act 3 is the logical playing out of the conflict you heaped up in Act 2.

Here you are with nine-tenths of a plotted-out book in your hands and you haven't even broken a sweat (I hope).

Up next—Act 1: Introductions.

16

ACT 1: INTRODUCTIONS

*** ✶ ✶ ✶ ***

THE HORN GAVE A CLEAR, COLD NOTE LIKE none I had ever heard before. There was a purity to that horn, a chill hard purity like nothing else on all the earth. It sounded once, it sounded twice, and the second call was enough to give even the naked men pause and make them turn towards the east from where the sound had come.

I looked too.

And I was dazzled. It was as though a new bright sun had risen on that dying day. The light slashed over the pastures, blinding us, confusing us, but then the light slid on and I saw it was merely the reflection of the real sun glancing from a shield polished bright as a mirror. But that shield was held by such a man as I had never seen before; a man magnificent, a man lifted high on a great horse and accompanied by other such men; a horde of wondrous men, plumed men, armoured men, men sprung from the dreams of the Gods to come to this murderous field, and over the men's plumed heads there floated a banner

I would come to love more than any banner on all God's
earth. It was the banner of the bear.

The horn sounded a third time, and suddenly I knew
I would live, and I was weeping for joy and all our spear-
men were half crying and half shouting and the earth was
shuddering with the hooves of those Godlike men who
were riding to our rescue.

For Arthur, at last, had come.

—Bernard Cornwell, *The Winter King*

If I've done my job right, Act 1 should almost write itself. You
already know how your book is going to begin, because we've
discussed your prologue. You already know how you're going
to bring your main character onstage the first time. You've even
written an introductory scene that can be adapted for use in Act
1. You've already envisioned how your hero's knot is affecting
her when the story begins. You already know how you'll introduce your antagonist and ticking time-bomb. You already know
what your setting and era and genre will be. You know what Act
2 constitutes so you know what you have to ramp up to. You
even know what the inciting incident will be.

Your first act is almost fully formed in your head *and you
haven't even written word 1.* As Kat says in Hilary Mantel's *Wolf
Hall,* "That's the value of an approach from behind."

What's left? A few new things, but most of what you need to
do is write the elements mentioned above.

WHAT IS ACT 1?

Act 1 is about introductions. Here you introduce not only your
hero and main characters but also your setting, genre, era, backdrop, villain, time bomb, stakes, theme, and more.

The burden of Act 1 is to prepare the reader to understand and enjoy Act 2. It's as simple (and as complex) as that.

Want us to care that your hero is in peril? Then you'd better introduce us to her and show us how she's someone we can root for. Want us to be concerned about an outbreak of disease near the hero's town? Then we'd better be shown the outbreak happening and its proximity to the hero. Introductions, introductions, introductions.

The contents of Act 1 might best be summarized by defining when it is you know you've reached the end of Act 1 and crossed over into Act 2. *Act 1 is complete when all the main characters have been introduced, when the main challenge of the story has been established, and when the hero has fully engaged the main challenge of the story.*

Let's look again at *Star Wars*. If Act 2 is the sequence inside the Death Star, then Act 1 is everything before that. Using the definition above, Act 1 ends when all the main characters have been introduced and the hero engages the main action of the story. The last main characters to be introduced are Han Solo and Chewbacca, so Act 1 can't end until after that. The story actually makes the departure from Act 1 easy to spot because it's the same moment the *Millennium Falcon* makes its departure from Tatooine and enters hyperspace on the way to adventure.

The main characters have all been brought onstage, we understand what the main danger of the story is, and the hero has engaged the action of the story: "There's nothing here for me now. I want to learn the ways of the Force and become a Jedi like my father." Cue dramatic music: dun-dun-dunnnnn. ...

Now Act 2 can begin.

In *The Lord of the Rings*, Act 2 begins after the Council of Elrond. We've met all the main characters, we have learned what the main danger of their predicament is, and Frodo has accepted the charge to take the Ring to Mount Doom, which is the main action of the trilogy.

In my first novel, *Virtually Eliminated,* the main character is a normal family guy and virtual reality programmer who has gotten caught up helping the FBI track down an online serial killer. Act 2 will be the one-on-one duel between our hero and villain. But Act 1 had a lot of setup to do to enable that duel. Indeed, the transition point from Act 1 to Act 2 comes almost at the midpoint of the novel, in terms of page count.

The end of Act 1 comes as our hero has come home to find his house on fire, with emergency personnel putting it out and tending to the wounded. He barrels upstairs to his son's room, smoke alarm blaring, where he finds that the villain has attempted to murder the boy. The FBI agent is on his heels. He's been trying to get our hero to sign on for real to go after this bad guy, but our hero's been resisting. Now our hero grabs an ax from a fireman's hands and chops it into the smoke alarm. "You give me what I ask for," he says to the FBI agent, "and I will bring this guy *down.*"

We've met all the main characters, we've seen what the danger and the situation is, and the hero has fully engaged with the main action of the story. End of Act 1.

Sometimes, like in that example, the hero engages the story. But sometimes the story engages the hero. In the movie *Alien,* Act 1 ends when we've met all the main characters, we've been introduced to the danger, and the alien bursts from Cain's chest and slithers away into the dark recesses of the spaceship. Now they are in a fight to the death with this creature whether they want to be or not. The story engaged them.

YOUR ACT 1

Let's think about your story now. You already know what your Act 2 is, so a large part of your task in Act 1 is simply providing whatever setup is needed to get Act 2 going.

Think about that bit in isolation. The first external event on your map of Act 2 may actually be something that happens in Act 1: the inciting incident. So let's step backward from there. What needs to happen so that readers can comprehend and feel the impact of the inciting incident?

In *Star Wars*, the inciting incident is when R2-D2 and C-3P0 roll into Luke Skywalker's life. But we couldn't just start there. Some setup had to be done first. We had to see that these droids were working for the good guys, that Artoo was carrying vital information, that a princess had been captured, and that an evil galactic empire would be coming after those droids. We also had to have met Luke, if only to show a few moments of his bucolic life, before these heralds entered with their call to adventure.

What about your story? What has to happen before the inciting incident will work? Just write down the obvious.

Let's say the inciting incident is that modern-day pirates attack a cruise ship and take seventy-five passengers and crew captive for ransom. You could just start the book with the pirate attack, but we would have no context and wouldn't care what happened. We wouldn't even know whether the pirates were bad guys or Robin Hoods. You'd be better served by setting up some things first.

We need to see that the characters are on an ocean liner. You could show that our hero is the events coordinator for an aging cruise ship about to be retired. It would be interesting to know that she loves her job but is longing for marriage and a normal life. We need to know that a massive storm is coming. You could show the pirates planning their assault of the ship. And so forth. *Then* we'd be ready for the pirates to attack.

What could it be for your book?

Take a look at the gap between the inciting event and the first escalation on your map of Act 2. What needs to happen to get from the first point to the second? Again, just write down the obvious. You're giving yourself an outline to follow.

The next task is to combine the shopping list of things that must happen to set up the inciting incident with the laundry list of things you already know you'll need to include in Act 1: prologue, main character introductions, etc. The amalgamation of the two lists constitutes what you must write in your Act 1.

I hope the to-do list you come up with doesn't put you off. When I write, it seems like my work consists largely of crossing off items on such a list: "introduce that he's left-handed," "have them talk about her previous boyfriend," "establish that he needs money in a hurry." But it's a to-do list in service of art. These are the brass tacks of creating a plot that works, a vehicle for your main character's inner journey.

Equipped with this list, you bring your creativity to the task of figuring out how to work them all in—while engaging your reader, advancing your hero's arc, and hopefully having fun.

What I'm giving you is a map of Act 1. All you need to do is connect the dots.

MAPPING ACT 1

As we did with Act 2, we're laying out a blueprint for Act 1. The maps for Acts 1 and 3 are actually much easier than the one for Act 2, because they're either ramping up to Act 2 or playing out Act 2.

Here are the elements that must be addressed or included in your Act 1:

- Prologue (if you're going to have one) in which you introduce your antagonist, the ticking time bomb, and/or the main menace of the story

- A scene bringing your main character onstage the first time (in such a way so as to reveal his essential characteristics, show how he's likable and sympathetic, show what it is he wants, and hint at his knot and initial condition)

- A scene or sequence establishing the protagonist's life before the main action of the story intrudes upon it

- An introduction of the main danger or challenge of the story (if you've done this in the prologue, then write another scene in which the hero learns of the danger or encounters the challenge)

- An introduction to genre (be sure no one will confuse your fantasy for a contemporary romance—by bringing in some recognizable elements to identify the genre: an elf, perhaps)

- An introduction to the era, setting, and backdrop (we need to find out where we are, *when* we are, and what's going on in the background)

- Some indication of the kernel of your story, the thing you find cool about it

- Some kind of introduction to your theme and message, however subtle

- If you haven't done so already, an introduction to your villain and the ticking time bomb (even if you *have* done so in the prologue, we'll need at least one major update about this in Act 1, probably more than one)

- The inciting incident (the main danger's invasion of the hero's world and the thing that sends him on a detour to inner transformation)

- An introduction of all your main characters (really, it's best if no new major characters enter the story after Act 1; nobody wants some Johnny-come-lately to end up saving the day or being the main villain; we want to know all the players from Act 1 onward)

- The main character's reaction to the inciting incident (his effort to quickly get beyond the irritating interruption in order to get back to his old dysfunction)

- The event that causes the hero to fully engage the main challenge of the story

- Anything else you need to do to get Act 2 enabled and ready to rumble

That's a tall order for Act 1, isn't it? And, since no one seems to know the origin to the idiom "a tall order," I'm going to make one up. I think it should be a restaurant term for a complicated food order. The poor short-order cook gets this order sheet from the waitress, but the order is so long and complex that she's taped two or three sheets onto one another so that when she sticks it into his order wheel hanging over his station, it reaches almost to the bottom of the window. It's a tall order.

But don't feel so overwhelmed that you hang up your spatula. If you've struggled with putting together a cohesive plot in your previous attempts, *this list will change that.* Now all you have to do is write each of those elements. Put meat on the bones. Most of it you've either already done or have at least envisioned.

THE BIG THREE

By my definition, Act 1 is over at that moment when all the main characters have been introduced, we understand the primary danger or challenge of the story, and the hero has fully engaged the main challenge of the story (or it has fully engaged her).

Let's look at those big three elements one at a time.

INTRODUCING THE MAIN CHARACTERS

Because you've been through chapters 8 and 13, you've probably already given some thought to how you want to bring your main characters onstage—your hero, certainly, and probably your villain. Hopefully you've at least cast your mind across the idea of how to introduce the other featured characters in your book.

Do you know who all your main characters are? It's quite possible you don't yet know. That's fine. We haven't stopped to think about it before. Why not come up with a starter list right now?

You will have come up with some of them as you've thought through Act 2. I mean, if you know that Act 2 is a fight between your hero's squad of warriors and an elite enemy squad, you've already got ten to fifty major and minor characters. You may not have thought much about their personalities, but you know at least that they'll need to be introduced in Act 1. You'll want to take the important ones through all or most of part 1 of this book to develop their characters fully. But the rest you can do less work on.

If you've had the idea to personify the old way and the new way in characters or groups, that's another set of characters you can add to the list of people to introduce in Act 1. Plus, if you know there will be a sidekick, a chief henchman, parents, UPS men, tavern wenches, or robot repairmen, add them to the list.

Take a minute to go through the list and think about how to introduce each one. Some will need extended introductions. Others can be introduced in a group, as when introducing the hero to the team in the locker room. Some will merit a special Han Solo–style introduction ("Sorry about the mess"), while others can just walk on. Keep *proportion* in mind. If a character is essentially a featured extra, don't give her an unforgettable seven-page introduction.

On the other hand, if you come up with an awesome seven-page introduction for someone you thought was going to be an extra, maybe you've stumbled upon a character who is willing herself into a larger role. Now, I'm not one to believe in the mystical idea that characters "take over" a story against the novelist's will. But I do believe that sometimes the corners of a novelist's mind will produce story events or characters that need to be there but for whatever reason hadn't yet occurred to the writer.

I also believe that when you know who a character truly is you will find her refusing to do certain things—in the sense that you realize such a person would never do such a thing.

Part of your task in Act 1 is to introduce your major characters. The rest of the book should be accomplished by these people (or creatures, depending on your genre). Show us who they are, help us know who we're really going to like or dislike, and you've accomplished a major chunk of Act 1.

INTRODUCING THE PRIMARY DANGER OR CHALLENGE OF THE BOOK

There is some danger or challenge in your book, or there is no book. Now, it doesn't come in the form of a horde of bloodthirsty barbarians (although, as the boy in William Goldman's *The Princess Bride* reminds us, "Murdered by pirates is good!"—at least in a novel). It can simply be the desire to make a team or pass a test or reach a destination.

We're talking about what it is that will provide the resistance to your character's quest or safety. It might be personified in a villain but it is often the larger power over which the villain sits. It might be the Nazis or the Empire or the Mob (or the feds). It might be a system that stands opposed to the hero. It might be a disease or caste system or corporation.

Take a look at your Act 2. What is the external source of all your hero's aggravations?

The appearance of this irritant or danger will happen in the inciting incident. But now we've got to expand it. It's got to move in en masse and show that it's here to stay and intends to cause as much trouble for the hero as possible, resulting possibly in her overthrow if nothing is done.

It's interesting to the reader in a sort of remote way to learn that the evil galactic empire is out there, but until it comes in and kills a character we like, we don't really care. It's good to know that ShanYu's army is swarming over the Great Wall of China, but it doesn't get to us until they burn a village and slaughter the inhabitants. It's one thing to see a cluster of tornadic cells on the Doppler, but until the cows start flying it's only an idea.

In *Virtually Eliminated,* mentioned previously, the hero theorized the existence of a bad guy killing people over a futuristic version of the Internet. It became real when he encountered this guy online. He spotted him, probed his defenses, even managed to win a little skirmish. Then the killer began probing back. Things started to escalate. The killer knew someone was on his trail, so he took measures to eliminate the problem. When that proved impossible, he attacked our hero's son.

Do you see how the danger is now fully established? It began with the inciting incident, but at that point it still seemed minor and remote to the hero. As Act 1 progressed, however, and more characters were introduced, the danger increased and became closer, more real. To the point where there was no denying it, no going back.

That's what you need to do in your story. You've already mapped out how the intensity escalates in Act 2. Now do the same for Act 1. The challenge seemed like no big deal at first, but more and more it encroaches and looms. It seemed transitory, but now that the hero has had a chance to examine it more carefully, it becomes clear that this is a substantial enemy that has no intention of leaving. How can you do that for your book? How can you escalate between the inciting incident and the real striving in Act 2?

Remember, your hero is only as heroic as the challenge she overcomes. Bring on a serious obstacle and make the hero all too aware that this is going to take everything she has to defeat it.

GETTING THE HERO TO FULLY ENGAGE THE MAIN CHALLENGE OF THE STORY

The final moment of Act 1 is when the hero decides, "Okay, let's do this thing." He crosses the Rubicon and turns to face the challenge, which he has now learned is a formidable one.

In Act II, Scene X of *Cyrano de Bergerac,* Cyrano meets the man his beloved Roxane is in love with. He's a dolt compared to Cyrano, but he's brave and, as Cyrano begrudgingly admits, he's handsome: "True, he's fair, the villain!" Watch the passage in which Cyrano hits upon his idea—which becomes the main challenge of the story—and fully engages it.

Cyrano: Roxane expects a letter.

Christian: Woe the day!

Cyrano: How?

Christian: I am lost if I but open my lips!

Cyrano: Why so?

Christian: I am a fool—could die for shame!

Cyrano: None is a fool who knows himself a fool. / And you did not attack me like a fool.

Christian: Bah! One finds battle-cry to lead th' assault! / I have a certain military wit, / But, before women, can but hold my tongue. / Their eyes! True, when I pass, their eyes are kind . . .

Cyrano: And, when you stay, their hearts, methinks, are kinder?

Christian: No! for I am one of those men—tongue-tied, / I know it—who can never tell their love.

Cyrano: And I, meseems, had Nature been more kind, / More careful, when she fashioned me,—had been / One of those men who well could speak their love!

Christian: Oh, to express one's thoughts with facile grace!. . .

Cyrano: . . .To be a musketeer, with handsome face!

Christian: Roxane is precieuse. I'm sure to prove / A disappointment to her!

Cyrano: *(looking at him)* Had I but / Such an interpreter to speak my soul! /

Christian: (with despair) Eloquence! Where to find it?

> Cyrano: *(abruptly)* That I lend, / If you lend me
> your handsome victor-charms; / Blended,
> we make a hero of romance!
>
> Christian: How so?
>
> Cyrano: Think you you can repeat what things / I
> daily teach your tongue?

And the game is afoot.

WALL-E has fallen in love with Eve and is taking care of her while she's been rendered inactive. Then a rocket arrives and draws Eve to it while WALL-E is away. Is he just going to let her go or is he going to try to stay with her? He races to the rocket and, just as it takes off, manages to attach himself to it. Now he's committed. He's all-in. Whatever happens, the rest of his life will be divided by that watershed decision to fully engage.

In my fifth novel, *Operation: Firebrand—Crusade,* my paramilitary team has gone to Sudan to redeem a girl stolen during a raid on her village and later sold as a slave. They manage to accomplish the distasteful transaction to buy her back, but along the way they've seen the state of affairs there. They've gotten a sense for the situation on the ground. They realize that there are thousands of other slaves not yet redeemed—and there's no guarantee that the raiders won't come back tomorrow and take this girl back into slavery.

So now they have a decision to make. They have realized the gravity of the situation and the pertinacity of the enemy. They've seen the vulnerability of the villagers. And here they are, a squad of highly trained, well-equipped covert ops specialists who just happen to be in the neighborhood. What's a body to do? Should they pack up and leave or stick around and see if they can turn hunter into hunted? You can probably guess what they decide. In that moment, they have fully engaged the main challenge of the story.

Luke decides to learn the ways of the Force. Frodo decides to take the Ring to Mount Doom. Erin Brockovich decides to take on PG&E. My hero in *Virtually Eliminated* decides to launch a campaign against the killer who tried to murder his son.

Alternately, Act 1 may end at the moment when the main action fully engages him. We saw that in *Alien*. We see it in *A Christmas Carol*. We see it any time the hero would rather sit this one out but is forced into the struggle anyway.

What will it be in your story? The main characters have all been introduced and the danger of the story has risen to a point where it cannot be ignored. Now you need that one last moment to come along and shove your hero into dropping her books and rushing into the fray. What will it be? What fantastic, awful, brilliant moment will it be when she dives in with both flippers?

In some stories, there is a definite moment when Act 1 ends. When the *Millennium Falcon* streaks into hyperspace, Act 1 of *Star Wars* is done. That's a great "whoosh" moment that acts like the curtains coming down to signal the change of acts.

Take a moment to think about your story. Brainstorm a few ideas for a great "Here we go!" bit that shows the hero and the story passing through the gate to realms unknown.

A last word about the big three: Don't worry about the length of your Act 1. Take as long as you need to get these three things accomplished. If that's half your book or more, who cares? There's no law that says the acts should divide your book neatly into three equal portions. My novels generally go like this:

- Act 1—nearly half the book

- Act 2—about a third of the book
- Act 3—about a quarter of the book

Yours can be like that or different. So long as you've gotten done the things I've covered in this chapter, you're fine.

ALMOST HOME

Right now you're like a construction team building a bridge across a river. You've got the foundation on one side (all the preliminary stuff in your "stew") and you've got the foundation on the other side (what happens in Act 2). What you're doing now is pulling these sides together. Each element becomes a pillar or beam spanning the gap between where the *book* begins and where the *story* begins.

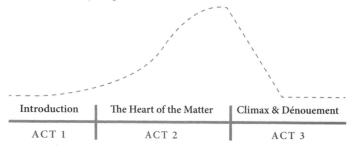

Introduction	The Heart of the Matter	Climax & Dénouement
ACT 1	ACT 2	ACT 3

Take a look at your Act 2. Think of the fun you're going to have writing the heart of the matter. Now ask yourself what needs to happen before that part can begin.

In *Nim's Island,* the real joy of the story is the middle, its Act 2, when Nim is defending her island, her father is trying to repair his boat and get home, and Alex Rover is trying to overcome her phobias and get to the island. But that story's Act 2 simply wouldn't have worked without the introductions provided by Act 1. First we needed to learn that Nim and her father live alone on this island no one knows about. We needed to learn that Alex Rover is a fear-ridden novelist who writes adventure stories but can't venture out to get the mail. We needed to see Nim's father get caught in a storm, leaving Nim by herself on the island. And we needed to see Alex and Nim make contact. With all that set up, the fun could begin.

If you've struggled to create plots that satisfy and resolve, I hope you can see how well-equipped you are now with this story. Figuring out your book's Act 2 is the key to the book (and knowing your main character's escalation phase is the key to figuring out your Act 2). Act 1 is just stage setting and introductions that let you go to town with Act 2.

And now you're almost home. You've mapped out two out of three acts, but in reality you're much further toward completion than you may realize. Act 3 is simply what has to happen, given Acts 1 and 2. When you do your the work up front correctly, as we've been doing so far in *Plot Versus Character*, your climax has a certain inevitability. If we can say that Act 1 almost writes itself when you know so much about it, then Act 3 grabs the keyboard and tells you to go grab a latte.

17

ACT 3: CLIMAX AND DÉNOUEMENT

★ ★ ★

"I AM GLAD THAT YOU ARE HERE WITH ME,"
said Frodo. "Here at the end of all things, Sam."
—J.R.R. Tolkien, *The Return of the King*

Now we come to it: the main event. What has gone before may be the heart of the book, but here we get the payoff. Plus fireworks.

Act 1 was all about setting things up for Act 2, the core of the tale. But inevitably, this story must come to a conclusion. On the inside, the hero is nearing her moment of truth. This must be reflected in the outside as well. External events have come to a head. The villain must finally be stopped. The romantic interest must not get away. The OR ELSE consequence looms large and is resolved for good or ill.

And then, live or die, win or lose, we must complete the story. We must have the falling action, the dénouement. We need to see who lived and died and whether the boy really did get the girl. We need to hand out medals and visit people in the hospital and tie off loose ends. We need to see how the main character is now, here in the rubble or confetti of the story's close.

Ah, the glory of Act 3.

GATHER YOUR ADVISORS

For all this time through *Plot Versus Character* you've been thinking out your novel. You've got a chapbook literally stuffed with ideas for Act 3, I hope, and should be feeling eager to get writing. At last you have not only a realistic main character but a incredible plot to show her off in!

As we arrive at the field where they're going to light the fireworks, let's pause to contemplate.

Where is your book going? What's left to do? How near to the moment of truth is your hero in her inner journey? What setting have you imagined for that to happen in? Could that setting be near or the same as the setting for your external climax in the story line? How would she get from one to the other? What is the status of the ticking time bomb? Why is the climax going to happen now? What is forcing it to be resolved one way or the other? What's the villain up to?

Just as your genre and era and villain and the rest suggest some things about your plot on the front end, so they may require or suggest certain elements here at the end of all things.

We'll get to brass tacks in a minute, but for now just write a paragraph summarizing what you want to be sure to do here at the big moment of your book. What things must happen here? What things do you still hope to do in this book? How could you hit your theme one last time here?

Later, when we've gotten much more specific about what goes into Act 3, be sure to come back to this paragraph to verify that you've included everything you wanted to include. If not, work it in.

Now … let's land this plane.

WHEN DOES ACT 2 END AND ACT 3 BEGIN?

Act 2 ends when everything is in place for Act 3. That sounds like a nonanswer, I know, but it will make sense in a minute.

Sometimes when I teach this material in writers' conferences I start at the climactic moment and work backward. I have writers envision what they want the titanic struggle at the apex of the story to be: Two combatants locked in strangleholds high above the city, aggrieved lovers trying to hurt one another while longing to reunite, fighter pilots in a desperate bid to stop the bomber before it drops its payload on the capital city. Then I say, "Okay, what has to happen before that can happen?"

We back up and see that there is a point at which everything is in place for the final assault, the last hurrah. All the elements have been established and the hero and antagonist have reached a point at which a collision is inevitable. That point marks the division between Act 2 and Act 3.

In this book I've started with Act 2, not the climax of the book, but you can still benefit from the exercise. Look at your map for Act 2. The last item on your list is probably the most serious blow yet to the hero's desire to overcome the challenge and go back to his old way. If the hero escalates one more time and decides to take out this menace once and for all, and if the challenge or antagonist escalates one more time, things are headed for an explosion.

What would that explosion look like? Describe what the final fight between hero and challenge might entail. The hero is trying one last do-or-die effort to achieve his goal, and the opposing force is preparing one last stroke to silence the hero at last. And if you've got a ticking time bomb going, this is when to count it down to its final seconds. The walls are collapsing, the water is rising, the fuse is almost spent, and there stand hero and villain eye to eye, locked in a fight to the finish.

Or, if you're writing a romance, it will look to all the world that there's no way the two of them can possibly reconcile. She's on a plane already taxiing on the runway—what's he going to do? Or she's walking down the aisle to marry someone else— what's he going to do?

Envision what your awesome end-all moment might look like, and then step back from it. What has to happen to set that moment up? Well, they've got to have a big last fight. She's got to get to the airport or the church. He's got to be far away from there. Then he needs to make the realization that he's got to get her back.

Or the hero's got to arrive at the place where the cutoff switch for the thermonuclear launch sequence is, which means he needs to have arrived at the control room, which means he needs to have infiltrated the facility, which means he needs to have arrived at the facility.

Stepping backward through the necessary setup steps is a great way to figure out where that final sequence begins. At some point you'll back in to the final element on your Act 2 map. The point where the last Act 2 thing has finished and the first setup for Act 3 begins is the point at which Act 2 ends and Act 3 begins.

For instance, let's look at our old standby, *Star Wars*. Act 2 has been the sequence inside the Death Star. That's a rough approximation. A more precise way to say it would be that Act 1 ended when the *Millennium Falcon* evaded the Imperial cruisers and jumped into hyperspace. At that moment, the curtain dropped on Act 1 and the heart of the movie was able to begin.

Act 2 began in their time in hyperspace, their arrival at the rubble of Alderaan, their chase of the TIE (Twin Ion Engine) fighter, and their discovery of and capture by the Death Star. Then they're inside the Death Star, fighting storm troopers, rescuing princesses, and getting back to the ship. Act 2 continued as they left the Death Star and fought the sentry ships. They had that long WW2-style battle and then finally blasted into hyperspace. The final moment of Act 2 was the revelation that the Empire had planted a tracking device on the *Falcon*.

The big climax of Act 3 in *Star Wars* is Luke's trench run, his mission to drop a proton torpedo down a tiny hatch and hopefully blow up the Death Star. It's a thrilling scene, with all the right kind of chaos and stress. But we couldn't jump directly from the *Millennium Falcon*'s escape to the trench run. Other things had to happen first.

In that sense, Act 3 is like the whole book in miniature. Just as you couldn't start the story at the best part but had to do Act 1 to establish and introduce things first, so you can't get straight to the climax as soon as you start Act 3. You have some things to get going first.

Act 3 of *Star Wars* begins when Luke and crew arrive at the secret Rebel base and begin their analysis of the Death Star schematics. It continues with the approach of the Death Star, the briefing of the pilots, and the departure of small fighter ships on what appears to be a suicide mission. All of this is setup for the climax. But even this isn't enough to get us to the big moment. To get to the trench run, we have to show the early portions of the battle, which include lots of explosions, heroism, and loss. Finally, things are ready for Luke's attack.

So it is with your book. You've already given some thought to what the final showdown will look like in your book. It may not be your final solution, but it's good for this exercise. If that is the climactic moment in your story, what would need to happen to set it up? I don't mean introduction of the characters or all the other stuff that readers will have already gotten by now, but what are the steps immediately preceding the climax? The last-minute maneuvering to get all the pieces into place so the final push can begin?

When you've hit on the very first step that leads directly into the climactic moment, you've found the place where Act 2 ends and Act 3 begins.

What is it for your book? Write it down.

Can you feel the downhill tilt to the road now? Here we go!

THE CLIMAX

Act 3 has two pieces: the climax and the dénouement. Each of those two portions has several items within. Let's talk about them in detail.

The climax of a novel actually has four components:

1. The run-up to the climactic moment (last-minute maneuvering to put the pieces in their final positions)

2. The main character's moment of truth (the inner journey point toward which the whole story has been moving)

3. The climactic moment itself (in which the hero directly affects the outcome)

4. The immediate results of the climactic moment (the villain might be vanquished but the roof is still collapsing)

Many times, all four of these will happen as a stand-alone set piece, a huge scene or series of scenes that constitutes the endgame.

Often, this is done in a location we haven't seen yet. In those cases, Act 3 is easy to identify.

Battles and monsters and betrayals have tried to bar their way, but Frodo and Sam finally arrive at Mount Doom. The whole Cracks of Doom sequence is the climax portion of Act 3 in the *Lord of the Rings* trilogy.

After all the ups and downs, the Nazis really are going to open the Ark of the Covenant. The entire cave sequence of *Raiders of the Lost Ark* is the set piece that comprises the climax portion of its Act 3.

The stolen plans have reached the Rebel Alliance and they launch a desperate attack to preserve freedom in the galaxy. The Death Star attack sequence is the climax portion of Act 3 in *Star Wars*.

Mulan has been disgraced but she must still somehow save the emperor from Shan-Yu's assassins hidden in the victory parade. The Forbidden City sequence is the climax portion of *Mulan*'s Act 3.

Alex and Sophie have written their song together and now Cora and Alex are going to perform it at the sold-out concert— but can Sophie even look at him anymore? The concert sequence is the climax portion of Act 3 in *Music and Lyrics*.

In these stories and more, there's an actual location element to Act 3. It's as if the set designers have built a special arena just for the final showdown. I actually quite like the feeling that the curtain fell on Act 2, the stage hands have taken off the old set and are preparing something new and wonderful, and then the curtain rises to show us the climax of the play.

But there's nothing that says your climactic moment has to be in a different location. If it's a sports story, for instance, the climax may take place in the same place much of the rest of the book has taken place: the court or field. If the characters have been trapped in an elevator for the whole book, the climax will most likely take place in the elevator. So long as you cover all the elements, you're fine. But why not take it to a new fun location?

Think about your story a moment. You may have a good idea for where the big showdown needs to happen, but you may not. And even if you've thought of a place, considering other options will help you find surprising wonders or can verify that you have, indeed, found the right place for this crucial action.

What is the ultimate setting for the final conflict in your book? If you're writing a thriller about a killer who preys on children, could the final standoff occur on a playground? If you're writing a romance about flirtatious ornithologists, could the final will-he/won't-he moment take place in the world's largest aviary? If it's a pirate story, the climactic scene had better be on the high seas. A fight at a local bowling alley just wouldn't cut it, you know? There's an appropriateness about your story regarding the "right" location for the big scene in your book.

My sixth novel, *Operation: Firebrand—Deliverance,* is all about the supposedly nonexistent concentration camps in modern North Korea. The climactic scenes don't take place in Laguna Beach or on a submarine. The climax takes place in a North Korean concentration camp.

Where is the perfect place for your book's climactic sequence?

Let's look at each of those elements.

THE RUN-UP TO THE CLIMACTIC MOMENT

Actually, you've already figured this out. When we started at the climactic moment and worked backward—that was the run-up. We did it then to determine when Act 2 ended and Act 3 began, but it's also a very useful first pass at the early portion of Act 3.

As I mentioned, Act 3 is the whole book in miniature. There's a beginning, middle, and end. Rising action, climax, and falling action. Things have to be set up for the big event, the big event happens, and then there is the fallout.

If your Act 3 takes place largely in a new location, the run-up begins when the hero arrives at the new location. So somehow you've got to get from the last item on your Act 2 map to this location. Maybe at the end of Act 2 your hero can set out for the Act 3 location: she heads to the launchpad, he runs toward the stables, she picks up her sword and strides toward the creature's lair.

If your Act 3 does not take place in a new location, you can still indicate the hero's intention to purposely walk toward the final confrontation. The "Let's roll" moment can be when the curtain comes down on Act 2.

Act 3, then, begins in the next logical point on that journey. He arrives at the airport. She reaches the underground silo. He blasts through the wall and begins his assault.

Now your Act 3 has begun. The rest of your task in this portion is to get him from that starting point to the climactic moment.

Again, it's a simple matter of connecting the dots. Well, once she enters the lair she'll have to do some looking around. She'll probably encounter guards of some kind, which she'll have to fight or outwit. She'll get deeper into the bowels of the den. We'll need lots of description of what she's seeing and smelling. Somehow she'll have to encounter something that leads her to the right place. Her goal will be in sight and she'll move toward it. But then of course the villain and his chief henchmen will appear. She'll deal with all the other obstacles and finally come face to face with the villain, who is about to do the dastardly deed that will doom the realm. She draws her sword and charges in!

Or, well, he gets to the airport and jumps out of his car. But because of his character, he can't bear the thought of going against the Department of Homeland Security, so he politely gets back in the car and finds a proper parking space and places his parking stub on the dashboard. Meanwhile the airline closes the door on the plane. She's on board! He runs across the parking garage and enters the terminal. He checks a screen to see what gate she's at and off he goes. And so forth, right on through to the climactic moment.

What will happen in your book? What are the final fine adjustments needed to set up the climax? Write them down.

See how this part is writing itself? After you make a few key decisions, everything else is a matter of servicing and enabling those decisions.

THE MOMENT OF TRUTH

Chapter 7 is entirely devoted to your main character's moment of truth, the peak of her inner journey, so I won't spend too much time on it here.

The main thing to do now is to integrate what you decided about her moment of truth with what you now know is going to be your Act 3.

Back in part 1, your plot was this ephemeral theory, but now it's got form and gritty detail. So take a look back at your notes for chapter 7. How was it you wanted to portray that breathless moment when your hero stands at the threshold, fully informed of how the old way is poisoning her and how the new way could help her, and decides which way to leap? How can you root that idealized moment into the context you've now created for Act 3?

Remember, the main character's moment of truth in her inner journey needs to take place late in the story but still before the external climax. This is because what she decides to do or become in her moment of truth affects how she will behave in the climactic moment.

If he's been a coward the whole time and now, with the villain about to make off with the treasure and the girl, he has a choice to make: man or mouse. If he decides to go with the old way and remain gutless, he'll probably escape his own danger, be rejected by the villain's henchmen as a coward, lose the girl and the treasure ... and hate himself forever. If he decides he's not going to crawl away one more time, then he'll face a new set of consequences for that choice. The villain and his men will fight him, he may still lose the treasure and the girl, but he will have done so as a hero.

What your main character decides in her moment of truth has everything to do with how the climax of the book plays out. It doesn't mean that if she makes the "right" decision she'll automatically win the day (though that is usually what happens), but it does tell you how she will act in the climactic moment of the external storyline.

So think now about your hero's moment of truth and how it might impact the climax of the novel. You've probably decided whether he'll choose the new way or the old way, so think about how that would look given the big walls-falling-down climax you're designing.

While you're at it, why not consider what it would look like if he were to choose the other way? If you've decided he'll choose the new way, go ahead and think about how it would go if he were to choose the old way instead.

At this moment in Act 3, probably more than anywhere else in your novel, the inner journey and the outer journey are interconnected. The "plot" that is the story of your character's internal transformation here intersects the outer plot that has made that transformation possible. The moment of truth decides it and the climax illustrates what she decides.

The best example I know to illustrate the moment of truth and its connection to the external climax is the story of the last hours of Jesus. Whether you believe it happened or not, it's a terrific story.

He was praying alone in the Garden of Gethsemane. He knew his "hour" was upon him. He had the choice to go through with the crucifixion or avoid it. It was his moment of truth. If he went through with it, no one would understand. It would look like a defeat—or, worse, a falsification of everything they'd come to believe about him. There would be torture, humiliation, and a sadistic execution. He could avoid it, however. He could just fly away or turn invisible or call twelve legions of angels to bust him out. But how then would his father's purposes be served?

What he decided there in the garden determined how he behaved in the events that came next. If he'd decided to use his power to escape, then he would not been there when the guards came to arrest him. Or he could've rendered them all blind or caused the earth to swallow them up. Instead—because he'd decided "Not my will, but yours, be done"—he simply allowed himself to be arrested. When his followers fought to protect him, he rebuked them and healed the one they'd injured. He stood silently before his accusers.

Everything he did in the external "plot," from the arrest to the trial to the crucifixion to the resurrection, was determined by what he decided in his moment of truth at the pivot point of his inner journey.

So it should be in your novel. Your hero's moment of truth determines her behavior in the climax.

THE CLIMACTIC MOMENT ITSELF

It's finally here, the moment we've all been waiting for: your chance to pull out all the stops and get a little crazy.

Because your characters will certainly be flirting with desperation bordering on temporary insanity. Like a pressure cooker about to erupt, it's all been building to this. Now it's time to blow everything up. Mwahahaha.

You've already taken early shots at envisioning this moment. Do you have any refinements now that you've thought through Act 3 more carefully? What is your external climax going to look like? Make it crazy. Turn up the heat until you don't think the story can bear it any more—then triple it!

Volcano erupting, lady giving birth, bomb ticking down, flood rising, car running out of gas on the tracks, train coming, allies falling to the sword on all sides. All novel long you've been heaping abuse on your hero to try to get her to change. Now it's your chance to grab two handfuls of grief and drop it on her head. Man, this is fun.

The more dire you make it for the hero here at the end, the more heroic you make her—and the more you engage your reader. If the whole book up to her moment of truth has been about getting her to contemplate a transformation, this part is *testing* her transformation. Okay, you've decided to be selfless, but do you really mean it? Will you hold to your commitment if I do … this?

Or maybe it's not a test of her decision; maybe it's just a seemingly impossible task that must be done with time running out. It's the last stand and the aliens are closing in. Good guys are falling like flies and the only hope for any of them to survive is for our hero to make it to the air lock and blow all the aliens away. Can he do it?

Keep your OR-ELSE firmly in mind here. Remind yourself of the stakes. If the hero doesn't X, the villain will Y. The climactic moment will be all about the OR-ELSE.

If you're writing a more gentle story that doesn't have aliens or evil masterminds about to destroy the world (though why anyone wouldn't want aliens and evil masterminds in his book, I can't fathom), you can still ramp up the tension in the climax.

At the end of *Never Been Kissed,* Josie is standing on the pitcher's mound with the clock ticking down. She has wounded her would-be boyfriend but has attempted to redeem herself by writing a confessional article for her paper. She hopes Sam will forgive her and come to the ballpark before the clock counts down to zero. Everyone in the crowd is right there with her, hoping he'll come, but there's no sign of him. She'll lose the one thing she most wants if he doesn't come. But he's not anywhere to be—wait, who's that? There he is!

That nail-biting moment didn't involve a single mutant, dragon, or zombie, but it did an excellent job of raising tension and producing an admirable climax to the story.

What will your story's climax be?

THE IMMEDIATE AFTERMATH

What happens right after the climax? I'm not talking about the falling action in which characters sit around drinking mint juleps. I'm talking about those seconds immediately after the climax has transpired, for good or ill.

The bridge is still going to collapse. The train is still going to crash. The recital is still going on. They're still surrounded by mutants *and* zombies. The main villain may have been defeated, but the walls that were falling down on the hero's head before are still falling down.

What needs to happen immediately after the climax?

Many new authors want to end the climactic scene as soon as the villain gets tipped into the bottomless pit, but that's a mistake. For the reader to get closure on the moment, you need to complete what you've started. You need to get the hero out of that dangerous place.

Show him grabbing the heroine's hand and sprinting out of the cavern just as it collapses. Show the hero clambering aboard a fishing vessel to be taken to safety. Show the hero stepping behind a concrete wall just as the house finally explodes.

Or, in those softer stories, show the boy finally hitting the home run. Show the woman nailing the high note. Show the man recovering the puppy at long last.

Play out the logical end of the scene that contained the climax.

What will that be in your story? After the hero does the big thing to save (or doom) the day, what happens immediately afterward? Resolve the moment.

When you've done that, you've finished everything that goes into the climax portion of Act 3. All that's left is to tie things off.

THE DÉNOUEMENT

The dénouement is the quiet recovery scene of your book. It's the happy celebration time when awards are bestowed and the couple gets married. The main danger of the book is gone—good, free people of the world have defeated it—and now we enter into our well-deserved time of peace.

Throw a parade. Hold a dance. Host a party. Strike up the marching band. Pass out the champagne. Remember the medal ceremony at the end of *Star Wars*? That's what I'm talking about. This is the time to smile again, to believe that, because of what we did here, tomorrow can be a day of hope.

Your reader needs this scene. She's been through the wringer too, and you owe her a celebration.

Now, if your story has a dark ending, you still need to write a dénouement. Show the disposition of things now that the crisis is over. The jackboots march through the flower garden, the gibbets are busy, and the black fleet sets sail to rule with terrible might.

Either way, your reader has earned a bit of closure and tying off. Your story needs it too.

Just as the climactic portion of Act 3 has four components, so does the dénouement. To complete your novel you must:

1. Show the main character's final state (the end condition after his inner journey)

2. Show the overall disposition of things now that the climax has passed

3. Tie off all loose ends

4. Suggest how things might be moving forward for the characters (including an indication that danger still exists, if you're setting up a sequel)

SHOW THE MAIN CHARACTER'S FINAL STATE

Because this was the topic of chapter 11, I'll not belabor it here. But I will recap.

Your main character has been through the fire. He's made a decision in his moment of truth that has not only affected how he behaved in the climax of the story but has left him a changed person. He's either a new man, full of hope and joy because he's chosen the new way, or he's ten times worse than he was at the outset. At the end of the book, you need to show this. You need to reveal what he's like—physically and emotionally—as a result of his journey.

Take the opportunity to craft a scene or moment that echoes the first time we met this person. Your final state scene needs to be a reflection of that first scene in which you revealed his knot.

How is he now? Consciously refer back to that scene, possibly by re-creating it to some degree, to give your story a nice sense of circularity and completion. Maybe have him presented with the same scenario or choice he faced at the outset, and this time show how he's changed. This time he *doesn't* walk into the bar or this time she *does* stop to help the homeless man.

Ebenezer Scrooge takes Tiny Tim into his arms and becomes his second father.

Find a place to reveal what he's like in this "after" state. This is the payoff for the inner journey. If the whole book is really about the main character's inner journey and the whole inner journey pointed toward the moment of truth, then this is the necessary results exhibition. "Wow," says the eager news reporter, "you've come all this way and made this paramount change. How do you feel?" (pointing microphone at your character).

So … how *does* she feel? How is she different? Show it here at the end of your book. When you do, the main story—the hero's journey—will be done. The rest is just housekeeping.

SHOW THE DISPOSITION OF THINGS NOW

It's important to reveal what has changed in the external plot now that the climax is over. Has the enemy army been driven to the river? Are the police rounding up the last of the villain's men? Is the hospital going to be able to reopen now? Have the fish returned to the once-blighted bay?

Has the Rebel Alliance survived to fight another day? Are the free peoples of Middle-Earth throwing off the last remnants of Sauron and Saruman's tyranny? Are those two knuckleheads finally going to get married (no, not Sauron and Saruman). Is the runaway bride going to run away again? Can Phil Connors finally enter the day after Groundhog Day?

Incredible things have happened in the world of your story. Much of it has been internal, hidden inside the heart of the main character. But a lot of it was external. Your reader wants to know how it's all going to shake out now that the main challenge (or danger) of the story is gone.

How about your story? When the dust settles, who is left standing? We saw Jimmy go down during the battle, but now we see him with his arm in a sling. He's going to be okay. We saw Susie get extracted from the rubble, but now we see her beaming in the arms of her daddy.

Show us how the world of the story will be now.

TIE OFF ALL LOOSE ENDS

In addition to who's injured and who's now engaged to whom and what has become of the fire ant menace, you may have some other things to tie off.

Earlier in the story, Tom wanted to go to college, but it could happen only if he got a scholarship. We pretty much forgot about it when the story got hairy, but at the end, why not have the mailman bring a letter announcing his full scholarship to the college of his dreams?

Early in *Sneakers,* the team talked about what they were going to do with the money they would earn from the job. Then the whole thing went south. But at the end, they had the opportunity to name their terms—so they each requested what they'd dreamed about earlier in the story.

Reach back into the story. Look for things discussed or even just mentioned, especially things characters were hoping for or fearing for the future. See if you can grant a payoff to those who made it to the end.

Trust me, your readers will remember the things you brought up but never tied off. Because inevitably it will be something they too had wanted in their own lives and will be watching for you to address. If you don't do it, they'll be upset.

In your story, what are the five to ten things you need to be sure to tie off at the end of the book? Of course the main character's inner journey and the external storyline. But what about minor characters and secondary storylines? What about things merely mentioned in passing? What about that old hound dog—is he okay? Now is the time to wrap everything up in pretty paper and tie a red bow on top.

SUGGEST HOW THINGS WILL BE

Project into the future a bit. Will the widow's children receive guaranteed college educations? Is your hero starting a new job working for the White House? Are all the swords being beaten into plowshares?

How are things going to be different now that the action of the story has resolved? This is different from showing how things are different immediately after the climax. This is showing what the future will be like.

If you're planning more books in the series, you may need to cut away from the victory celebration to show that danger still lurks out there. It may have suffered a terrible defeat, but it's not finished. It will go away and nurse its wounds, and then it will return. And this time, it will strike first at the hero. Or whatever.

Darth Vader's TIE fighter rights itself and flies away. He'll be back. An alien seedpod evaded the scan. We haven't seen the last of them. The chief henchman didn't die. Now that the hero has conveniently dispatched the villain, the henchman can become the new top man. He'll be back, and with an army this time.

It doesn't have to be a sign of danger. If you want to imply that more adventure awaits, interupt the happy party with a phone call. "It's the Mayor. A new crisis has arisen!" Oh, boy, here comes more fun!

Note that these zingers can sometimes give your book an unresolved feel. You want that if it's a series. You want the reader to know that one major disaster was averted but another may soon need to be dealt with, though surely the heroes can have a short vacation first. But if it's not a series, you don't want the book to feel unfinished—or the reader to feel uneasy. If there's no good reason to suggest that more danger lurks in the shadows, I recommend you neatly tie things up. Let the book feel complete and resolved.

YOUR BOOK IS PLOTTED

You've done it, my friend. You've started with a blank page and a vague thought and now you have a complete map for your book's plot. If you've ever struggled finding structure for your story, I hope you've now found the solution.

It wasn't too difficult a pill to swallow, I trust. We started with character so you'd feel comfortable—and so your book would be character driven. Or plot-and-character balanced, which is the gold ring. While the maps we've produced of Acts 1, 2, and 3 may make you wonder if we've taken some of the spontaneity out of the process, I assure you that's not the case. What we've developed is an easy step-by-step process that will let you glide right through the writing process. And it's a bare outline. There will be plenty of room for spontaneity as you decide how to flesh it out.

All that's left for us to do is tie off a few loose ends of our own. One more chapter and we're done.

Part 3

PLOT AND CHARACTER

TOGETHER AT LAST

Novelists who come up with story ideas easily tend to look at character creation as a chore akin to grouting the bathroom. Other novelists, who in the course of a normal day meet fascinating fictional people who demand to be written, often look at plot creation with trepidation. They know it's something they probably have to do but they feel woefully inferior to the task.

My goal with *Plot Versus Character* has been to help both groups. The title is meant to be playful: It's plot in one corner and character in the other. Certainly the novelists who do one or the other better tend to see "the other" as the enemy, or at least look upon it with suspicion.

In reality, of course, the two aren't opposed at all. Just as a tennis player with a strong forehand but a weak backhand will never rise above the level of an amateur, so it is in fiction. As a novelist, you know instinctively which of the two you do better. You want to improve what you're already good at, true, but the thing that needs the most attention is the one you're not naturally strong in. Only when both are strong will your "play" be what it can be.

In our last chapter together, let's look at how this whole system works together.

18

INTEGRATING PLOT
AND CHARACTER

★ ★ ★

FIRST BING CROSBY STARTS OUT SINGING IN HIS
signature crooner voice:

> *Won't you play a simple melody*
> *Like my mother sang to me?*
> *One with good old-fashioned harmony*
> *Play a simple melody*

The song itself is simple. Slow and easy, like a child's song. But it's a
catchy tune and has a rolling rhythm you just can't help swaying to.

Then Gary Crosby, Bing's son, takes over. He sings a jaunty
stanza in ragtime style:

> *Musical demon, set your honey a-dreamin'*
> *Won't you play me some rag?*
> *Just change that classical nag*
> *To some sweet beautiful drag*
>
> *If you will play from a copy of a tune that is choppy*

You'll get all my applause
And that is simply because
I want to listen to rag

Now the instruments take a turn. Trumpets play a bright bridge between the verses. Then the real fun begins: Bing and Gary repeat their verses—singing their very different tunes together.

At first it doesn't seem like it will work. Maybe it's a mistake—one of them came in too early. Then … magic. You suddenly realize the melodies are two pieces of the same whole. One fast, the other slow, but perfectly synchronized. Before the verse is over, the song almost can't be imagined without both parts, and the rest of the experience is bliss.

Can you guess the writer of this, one of the first true counterpoint songs in American music? None other than our old friend Irving Berlin. (Search YouTube for "Bing and Gary Crosby—Play A Simple Melody" to hear it for yourself.)

Both parts of this song work. They stand alone quite nicely and, if that's all that had ever been done, it would've been fine. But when they are put together, each part doing its own thing in its own way yet working in partnership with the other, it becomes something special. Elevated.

So it is with the novel you've planned during our time together.

You came to the process with one melody already singing beautifully in your mind. Had you written the book with just that part, the result would've been fine—workmanlike, even. But it wouldn't have had the magic of Berlin's "A Simple Melody." It would've been, in a word, forgettable.

But because you seek that same elevation we hear in this song, you have come to *Plot Versus Character* to teach yourself counterpoint, to add to what you can already do that thing you haven't yet learned to do. The result is a more robust music that can be presented to a much wider audience.

As I've discussed both the creation of character and the creation of plot, I've done so in isolation, taking first one and then the other. But all along the idea has been for them to work in counterpoint.

We've already glimpsed some ways in which the main character's inner journey and the external story of the plot intersect, but in this chapter I want to make that explicit. Then we'll look at several stories to see how their character arcs and plot progressions work in harmony. I'll also discuss exceptions and special situations.

PLOT AND CHARACTER—THE BEGINNING OF A BEAUTIFUL FRIENDSHIP

We've been mapping so much in our time together that we've become regular cartographers. So on page 247 there's a new one to give an overview of how your main character's inner journey works in conjunction with your external plot.

The left side of the map shows your main character's inner journey. The right side shows the plot.

See how they connect? The first time you bring your main character onstage you're going to depict her initial condition and hint at her knot. See how that event bridges both sides of the chart? After establishing normal, you can violate normal through the inciting incident. The thing that marks the division between Act 1 and Act 2 is when all the main characters have been introduced, the main challenge of the book is revealed, and the hero engages that main challenge.

But even before Act 1 ends, the hero is in the early stages of an escalation phase between the old way and the new way. It began at the inciting incident and goes right on through the

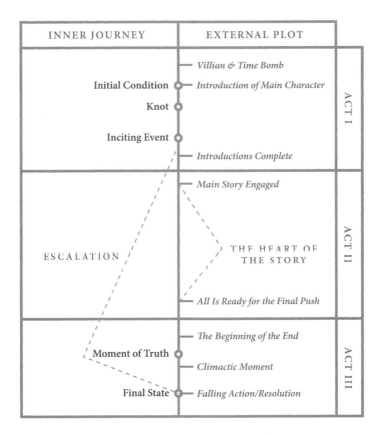

INNER JOURNEY	EXTERNAL PLOT	
	Villian & Time Bomb	
Initial Condition	Introduction of Main Character	ACT I
Knot		
Inciting Event		
	Introductions Complete	
	Main Story Engaged	
ESCALATION	THE HEART OF THE STORY	ACT II
	All Is Ready for the Final Push	
	The Beginning of the End	
Moment of Truth	Climactic Moment	ACT III
Final State	Falling Action/Resolution	

middle of the story. That roughly corresponds to Act 2, the heart of the matter. While the hero is growing more and more desperate to get back to her inner dysfunction, her outer world is getting more dangerous and complicated as well. The pressure mounts, inwardly and outwardly. Every time she tries to overcome an external obstacle (which is actually a counterattack by her internal "new way" foe), it comes back and escalates again.

Finally, everything is in place for the last standoff between the hero and the source of all her challenges and conflicts. Act 3 puts the players in their places and lets the fun begin. The hero has reached the breaking point in her inner journey. Through all the failures of this novel, she has come to realize how the old way has been hurting her and what the new way can do for her. In a singular silence she faces her moment of truth. Which way will she go? This is the moment when angels creep to the edge of heaven and peek down to see what she'll choose.

She makes her decision.

Then, her choice made, she goes to face her last challenge. What she does here is completely based on what she decided internally in her moment of truth.

The walls fall down. The missile is launched. The hero and villain crash about the lair in a fight to the death. Everything (externally) hangs in the balance. This is the climactic moment of the external storyline.

Ultimately, the climax is resolved. The hero gets out just in time.

And then, resolution. Dénouement. Who lived? Who got promoted? Who's finally caught and given his comeuppance? And how is our hero now, having made that choice in his moment of truth? What's his final state? Tie off loose ends, suggest what the future will be like, and maybe show there's more wrongs to be righted. Then: "The End."

There's your book, in a nutshell.

IT'S NOT A FORMULA

One reason I didn't trot out this chart early in the book is that I didn't want it to seem like I was giving you a formula for fiction.

Those formulas are available, you know. By page 30 you must have the first complication. By page 75 you have the reversal. And so on. Recurring plot devices and stock characters permeate formula fiction. Romance fiction is often accused of being formulaic.

Harlequin novels almost always have a resourceful but weak woman in need of rescue (from bad guys, a bad job, hardship, etc.). The first chapter will introduce an antisocial hero with bad people skills but a heart of gold—and a deep wound. Think Alex Karev in *Grey's Anatomy* or Sawyer in *Lost*. The rest of the book shows how these two will fight, flirt, and marry, at which point the woman will be saved from her peril and the man will suddenly open up and talk about his feelings.

Some might say that even by suggesting you write in any given genre, I'm telling you to write formula fiction. I contend that a genre is a genre because many people love the recurring settings and elements of these books, but that there is much room for variation within those parameters, as any comparison of *Twilight* and *Nosferatu* would reveal.

No, this isn't a formula. But it is a foundation. It's a set of best practices. It's a structure upon which you may build any story you please, examine any theme you choose, explore any setting or story type you like, and have any ending you want. How can something that open-ended be a formula?

What it is, is a construction kit. A box of LEGO blocks. So long as you include *something* in each spot on that chart, you will have a satisfying, page-turning story that honors realistic characters and wonderfully blends plot with personality.

SYNTHESIS ON PARADE

Now let's look at a few stories and see why they work on both sides of the chart. You'll note that not every story perfectly fits the map. That's okay—for you too. There's wiggle room here. Just be sure to include the biggies.

Note that the following summaries contain spoilers. If you haven't read the book or seen the movie being described, and you plan to, skip to the next one.

Cue the ragtime band.

Nim's Island

The whimsical opening of this story introduces in the form of a child's storybook that the heroine is a young girl whose mother has died and who now lives alone with her father on a deserted island. The girl's knot is her grief over the loss of her mother. We also come to meet Alex Rover, both in the form of the author and the heroic adventure hero she writes. Then Nim's father sails off on one of those ill-fated "three-hour tours" that always go so badly in fiction. Nim and Alex strike up a conversation via e-mail.

The storm hits and Nim loses contact with her father. That's the inciting incident for both protagonists: Nim and Alex. It is for Nim, because she knows she's alone and she calls for help to Alex. And it is for Alex, because she must now decide whether or not to leave the apartment her phobias have kept her trapped inside and try to be more like her heroic character and go help this girl on the other side of the world.

When Alex makes it out the door and into the taxi (hilariously, I might add), Act 1 ends. She has now fully engaged the main challenge of the story, we have met all the main characters, and we know what the major challenge is going to be.

Act 2 shows the struggles of our three major characters: Nim, Nim's father, and Alex. Nim struggles with her fear and loneliness and has to "defend her island" against a cruise ship full of tourists thinking they've found their own private island. Nim's father struggles to survive the storm and then repair his boat to get home to his little girl. And Alex has the biggest struggle of all:

overcoming all her phobias and neuroses to become the action hero she's until now only written about. She doesn't want to be brave. She'd rather go back to her safe apartment. But this new way, this desire to help a child, simply won't leave her alone.

Finally things are ready for the final push. Alex has gotten to a cruise ship but can't make it to the island. Nim's father has had his repaired ship's motor destroyed again. And Nim is feeling utterly alone. Either they all make it through this final challenge or all is lost. Alex hears from a boy on the cruise ship that there really is an island and there really is a girl alone there. That's all she needs. She's off to reach Nim's Island, come what may. That's the end of Act 2 and the beginning of Act 3.

Act 3 is Alex's escape from the ship's crew. She's rowing away in a stolen lifeboat—in the storm … at night. Quite a contrast from the agoraphobic in Act 1. She fights storm and surf and then, in sight of the island, she goes into the drink and nearly drowns. That is the climactic moment of the story.

In the end, Nim's father makes it back and is reunited with Nim. He also meets Alex Rover, who happens to be an attractive, intelligent unmarried woman about his age who already has a connection with Nim. The falling action is the suggestion that Alex will stay on with them and that together they will form a new family.

Had this crisis never come, Alex would have remained trapped in her fears. The story is called *Nim's Island* but Alex's transformation is really the point.

Operation: Firebrand

My fourth novel is the first in a series about a small, privately funded team of mostly ex-special forces operatives who go into the world's hot spots on missions of mercy.

The prologue is rather long in this book. It shows our hero, a Navy SEAL sniper, Jason, on patrol in Indonesia with his platoon and the mission that goes horribly wrong, leaving his best friend dreadfully wounded.

We learn that Jason's friend is paralyzed from the waist down and completely blames Jason for it. Our hero quits the Navy and takes a job cleaning sea scum off the bottom of boats in the San Diego Bay. He feels this is what he is—sea scum—and what he deserves. His crippling guilt is his knot.

Months later, Jason is approached by someone putting together a unique team of ex-special forces experts to do covert missions of mercy. The letter he receives inviting him to come check it out is the inciting incident. It sends him on this whole detour that will ultimately force him to choose between the old way (succumbing to his guilt) and the new way (using his skills for humanitarian causes).

He goes through the interviews and meets the other team members (introducing the major characters), but ultimately refuses to join. The new way (personified by the millionaire forming the team), however, is persistent. The offer escalates, as do his efforts to avoid entrapment. When it becomes clear Jason is not going to get out of this without physically hurting someone— and when he realizes that going on what are essentially suicide missions will probably result in his death, the thing he actually desires—he agrees to join the team. That's the end of Act 1.

Act 2 is Jason's attempt to pull this team together. They don't like each other, and he has at least one rival for the team's leadership position. There are female members of the team, and sexual tensions arise. Meanwhile, a revolution in Kazakhstan begins, putting an orphanage in direct danger. An American aid worker is captured, and this triggers the call for aid that eventually reaches our millionaire and calls the team into motion.

On the ground in Kazakhstan, the team discovers that some of the children have survived and are in hiding. They also learn that the American aid worker is being held by the insurgents. Battle rages all around, the Russian special forces and regular army are closing the gap around the urban combat zone, and time is running out. Somehow they've got to get these kids out of Dodge.

When the team locates a wagon big enough to transport all the kids, Jason comes to his moment of truth. He can go with them and get the kids out, choosing the new way that works for all that is good. Or he can attempt to save the aid worker, though leading the team there would compromise the mission and risk the orphans. Another option presents itself: He could go all out Rambo and try to rescue the aid worker himself. An action that would, he hopes, result in his death. This is what he decides to do.

Do you see that he basically chose "wrong"? He chose the old way, the way of destruction. Don't be afraid to at least contemplate letting your hero choose the dark path in his moment of truth.

I won't tell you all of what happens, but Jason is given yet another moment of truth. He eventually chooses the new way and uponda the root of the climax doing his best to rescue the children and his team.

The dénouement shows Jason more at peace with himself than he's been since the book began. He's chosen the new way and it suits him. He agrees to stay on with the team, this time for real, not so he can find a way to kill himself. His future looks hopeful and there is even the prospect of romance in the air. Plus more adventures to come, of course.

Titanic

One more analysis. This time the movie *Titanic*.

The first time we see Rose, our main character, she's already being controlled by her wealthy fiancé. She's obviously rich and well-to-do, but there are subtle signs that Cal is attempting to corral her and that she's resisting. Right away, we get a hint of her knot: She's bridling under someone's control and yet remaining under that control for some reason.

Of course the whole movie is a ticking time bomb. We know that as soon as she sets foot on that ship, she's consigned to a deadly future. There is a sweet agony about this. Every second of screen time in this movie subtly ratchets up the tension because we know they're getting closer and closer to that iceberg.

As we follow Rose in her "normal," we see more of her discontent with her situation. She longs for something beyond the hypocrisy and arrogance of the wealthy, but what option does she have? This is her knot. Rose is forced to be something she isn't. The old way says to keep playing the lie. The new way urges her to leave it all behind and be true to herself.

The cognitive dissonance threatens to tear her apart. Rose flees a dinner party, intent upon throwing herself overboard. There, she encounters Jack, who talks her down. This is the inciting event. Jack is everything Rose longs to be: free, artistic, unfettered. Though he is poor, he is happy.

Act 1 ends here. All the main characters have been introduced, we understand the hero's main challenge, and we get the hint that she will be investigating Jack Dawson in much finer detail.

Act 2 is Rose's growing desire to be with Jack, despite all the reasons for her not to be. Both the old way and the new way are personified: Cal and Jack, respectively. Cal increases his efforts to win her into giving her heart to him. He's willing even to bribe her into it, by giving her—no accidental naming, here—the heart of the ocean, a beautiful diamond. For his part, Jack escalates his efforts to be with Rose. Rivalry between Cal and Jack increases. You can just feel Rose teetering between desire and duty. It's a marvelous inner journey on display.

Throughout Act 2 Rose has several moments of truth. Almost every time, she elects to go with the new way—by running off with Jack to various trysts. She becomes bolder and bolder in her defiance of Cal, which causes him to increase his pressure, resorting even to violence, to get her to conform to his wishes.

In the external story, the ticking time bomb finally goes off. The ship hits the iceberg. When the ship begins to sink, Act 2 ends.

Act 3 is the whole set piece of the sinking of the *Titanic*. While the walls begin to fall, Rose's decision about whether to go with Jack or Cal is set before her. Cal will buy his and her way aboard a rescue craft, while Jack has been chained to a pipe in a deck that is about to flood. This is Rose's moment of truth. She decides to throw off the old way and go with the new way, even if it costs her her life.

The rest of Act 3 is purely the action component. How Rose behaves here—rescuing Jack and then trying to get off the ship with him—is all decided by what she chose in her moment of truth. If she'd chosen another way, she'd have just rowed away with Cal. Miserable and guilt ridden, but alive. Cal himself flips out and attempts to kill both Jack and Rose. Many shenanigans ensue.

The dénouement is many years later as she's recounting this story to a crew of listeners. She reveals that she has kept the diamond, which she now casts into the sea. Her heart is still in the ocean, with Jack.

ANALYZE THAT

You can see that none of those stories fit the model perfectly. Some moved the moment of truth to a much earlier point in the story. Some had it happen more than once. Some had ticking time bombs and some didn't. Some had prologues and some didn't. But all of them followed the basic structure I've presented.

That's freeing for you. I hereby give you permission to change the structure too. The largest blocks were there every time, and should be in yours, but there is freedom to tinker with the order (or even presence) of some of the elements.

Now that you understand the whole structure, I suspect you'll begin seeing it in the books you read and the movies you watch. Or you'll be able to think about them later and analyze them. You'll go, "Ooh, that's his old way coming back to claim him." Or "Hey, wait a minute, they didn't establish normal before violating normal—I don't care about any of these people yet!"

Now thou art unleashed on an unsuspecting world of literature and entertainment. Be afraid. Be very afraid.

INNER JOURNEYS AND MULTIBOOK SAGAS

Let's talk about some exceptions and special situations now.

It's all well and good to plan a full inner journey for a character who is going to be in only one book. But what about when you're beginning a series? Does he have to forget everything at the start of book 2 and go through it again? Does he need another knot? Can't he just be "fixed" and go on with his derring-do?

There is a variety of ways to handle this. One is to cover a different character's inner journey in book 2. In my *Operation: Firebrand* series, book 1 is about Jason's journey. Book 2 is about

Rachel's. Book 3 is about Chris's. The series may one day extend to six or even eight books. That's because I have six team members and two important characters who don't go on missions. Each one can have a book about his or her inner journey.

Another way to deal with this is to plan a larger arc for your main character. If you know that she's heading for such a total transformation that in book 1 she's going to be a pious saint and book 5 she's going to be a mass murderer, each book becomes a step on that journey. We've seen how one book can have multiple little moments of truth. Why can't a series be comprised of those smaller moments, with each book in the series covering one of these little achievements leading to her ultimate demise?

The larger *Star Wars* saga, which covers Anakin Skywalker/ Darth Vader's rise and fall and rise is a great example of a slow inner journey done over multiple external plots.

Another solution is to simply not have an inner journey at all, or to not have one after the first book. While its always nice to have a character dealing with an inner struggle, some characters face exterior challenges only—Indiana Jones or James Bond, for example. They stay pretty much the same in each installment of their respective series. While I recommend giving your main character an inner journey, establishing a larger-than-life hero that the rest of your story revolves around is another option. In these instances it's a good idea to have other characters who bring some internal conflict to the story.

STARTING WITH PLOT INSTEAD OF CHARACTER

I've saved this one for last. When you're creating a novel from scratch, you can do it exactly as I've described in *Plot Versus*

Character. But sometimes you don't have that luxury. Sometimes the plot comes to you first and practically intact, or you are otherwise constrained, and can't really build from the foundation up.

For instance, I was once assigned the task of rewriting a novel that had been written by a celebrity. The publisher knew the book was in trouble but needed to bring the book out to maintain good relations. They wanted me to salvage as much of it as I could, while still improving it.

In that case, I wasn't free to throw everything out and start over as I would've liked. The main plot was already in place and had to remain. It was as if I'd been given a house and told I could remodel it. I could tear down just about any internal walls I wanted, but the external structure couldn't be touched. It was quite a different challenge from writing a book beginning with nothing but a blank screen.

The first thing I did, after reading it, was begin working on the main character's inner journey. My mission was this: create for him a meaningful character arc that nevertheless caused him to do all the main things the plot needed him to do. It was not ideal, but it was a great puzzle to attempt.

You may be in that situation yourself. Maybe you've got this amazing idea for a plot and you simply can't deviate from it. Maybe you're depicting actual events, so there's no license for changing things. More likely you've actually written the whole book and are only now realizing you have no inner journey for your hero.

Never fear! You can gut the story, retain what you love about it, and also give it a fabulous inner journey for your main character. It's just going to be harder.

Start by listing the elements of the plot that absolutely cannot change. These are the nonnegotiables. Somehow you've got to work within their parameters. But you've probably already found several parts of the story that can be modified or replaced. This is where you'll find your wiggle room.

With those nonnegotiables in hand, begin thinking about what moment of truth someone in this situation could have. Given this climactic moment, what could've caused the hero to behave how she did? If she'd decided differently, how would the climax have played out?

From there, work backward.

Remember how I started the discussion of the inner journey by talking about the moment of truth? That will help you here. You can start going through the book in order now, beginning with that known point and then projecting back to knot, initial condition, escalation, and final state. Be sure to do the root personality work and other core character homework to arrive at a realistic personality.

You're doing much of the process backward, but you're still doing it. As you're working on this unusual situation, use this book as a resource, jumping around to whatever section you need at the time.

I've purposely saved this discussion for last because I wanted you to know the whole book and the whole system before granting permission to needle drop around in it. But now that you do know the full structure, you can jump about to whatever part will help you next.

CONCLUSION
* * *

WHICH COMES MORE NATURALLY TO YOU: CHARAC-
ters or plot? By now, you probably know the answer very well.

Understanding that you're a card-carrying member of
one group or the other is actually very helpful, as is most self-
understanding. When you know where your strengths are and
are willing to admit and work on your weaknesses, you're well
ahead of most of your peers. It takes real exertion to improve in
an area you're not naturally strong in.

I used to teach a cognitive training system that actually exer-
cised the brain like a muscle. Kids and adults came in struggling
to read or concentrate or process quickly, and we'd put them
through their paces: a rigorous regimen of strength-building
exercises. With some kids, mainly teens, it was at first a genuine
struggle to get them to keep their noses to the grindstone. But
when they saw the first improvement—when they suddenly knew
the answer before their classmates or their homework was suddenly completed in a fraction of the time they'd needed before—
they'd be sold. Then I'd have to hustle to keep up with *them*.

And I predict that's how it will be with you. You came to this
book, which means you're dedicated to improving your craft.
That's something that puts you ahead of your peers. And you've
stuck with me through a book that, at times, may have felt like it
was stretching you in new places. That's good. As it should be.

But the first time you see improvement in your fiction, you'll
be hooked. You'll realize that you—*you*—have created a genu-

inely interesting three-dimensional character, perhaps for the first time in your life. Or you'll see that *you* have been able to wrap your beloved character in a story that actually makes your teenager stay up late reading it. Yowza.

And when that happens, watch out, world. You'll be, as Irving Berlin might say, "Puttin' on the Ritz."

I can't wait to see what you will achieve when your plots and characters unite in perfect harmony.

INDEX

✴ ✴ ✴

ACKNOWLEDGMENTS

I HAD GREAT FUN WRITING THIS BOOK. ALONG THE way I occasionally needed help with ideas for excerpts or metaphors or examples, and I had even more fun calling upon my friends, most of whom are novelists themselves, for aid.

Thanks therefore go to Lyn Cote, Jill Williamson, Trish Perry, Nancy Mehl, Jenny B. Jones, Kathy Fuller, Susan Davis, Sharon Hinck, Robin Lee Hatcher, Sharon Dunn, Sherrie Lord, Stephanie Grace Whitson, Deborah Raney, Susan Davis, Gayle Roper, Austin Boyd, Angela Hunt, and Rick Marx (who is not a novelist but who loves science fiction).

Thanks to Kelly Nickell and Jane Friedman for getting excited about the idea and letting me pitch a book that wasn't on the list.

Thanks to Scott Francis for his excellent editorial insights and for getting my humor but not allowing me to go overboard with it.

Thanks to Jessica Boonstra for her brilliant and beautiful cover design. How *does* one depict the idea that plot and character go together? I'm glad the challenge was given to you and not me—you succeeded brilliantly.

Thanks to James Scott Bell for putting in a good word for me and helping with excerpts, metaphors, and many other things besides, and for friendship.

And thanks to Dianne E. Butts for sending me to the link that started this whole thing rolling.